Guardians of the Whales

Guardians of the Whales

THE QUEST

TO STUDY

WHALES IN THE WILD

BRUCE OBEE AND GRAEME ELLIS

ALASKA NORTHWEST BOOKS™

Anchorage • Seattle

Published by arrangement with Whitecap Books,
1086 West 3rd Street, North Vancouver, British Columbia, V7P 3J6.

Edited by Elaine Jones
Photographs by Graeme Ellis
Additional photography by Bruce Obee pp. 18, 42, 50, 55, 68, 71, 120;
John Ford pp. 78, 84, 87, 90, 94, 114, 115; Jim Borrowman pp. 81, 116;
Steve Swartz pp. 93, 97, 98, 101, 104, 109, 110, 119, 124;
Dave Myers pp. 113, 130; Mark Fraker pp. 128, 129.

Cover design by Warren Clark
Interior design by Carolyn Deby
Typeset at CompuType, Vancouver, B.C., Canada
Map by Dana Dahlquist, Dahlquist Axe Design and Communications Ltd.,
Victoria, B.C.

LIBRARY OF CONGRESS CATALOGING-IN-PUBLICATION DATA

Obee, Bruce, 1951-
  Guardians of the whales : the quest to study whales in the wild /
by Bruce Obee ; photographs by Graeme Ellis.
    p. cm.

  Includes bibliographical references and index.
  ISBN 0-88240-428-8

  1. Whales—Research—Pacific Coast (North America).   I. Title.
QL737.C4017 1992
599.50451′0979—dc20   92-15419
                                                                        CIP

Printed and bound in Canada by D.W. Friesen & Sons Ltd., Altona, Manitoba

The publisher acknowledges the assistance of the Canada Council and the Cultural Services Branch of the government of British Columbia in making this publication possible.

Alaska Northwest Books™
A division of GTE Discovery Publications, Inc.
22026 20th Avenue S.E.
Bothell, Washington 98021

For Michael Bigg,
a man of vision and conviction
whose spirit lives on

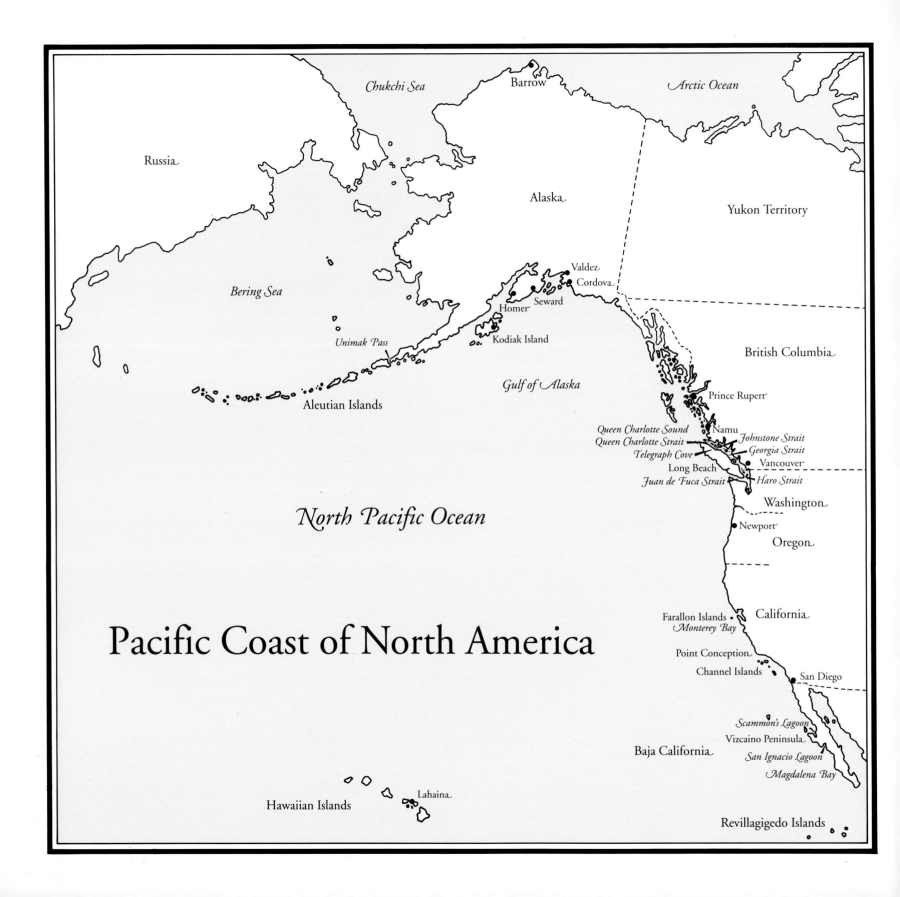

Chukchi Sea

Barrow

Arctic Ocean

Russia

Alaska

Yukon Territory

Bering Sea

Valdez
Cordova

Seward

Homer

Unimak Pass

Kodiak Island

British Columbia

Gulf of Alaska

Aleutian Islands

Prince Rupert

Queen Charlotte Sound   Namu
Queen Charlotte Strait   *Johnstone Strait*
Telegraph Cove   *Georgia Strait*
Long Beach   Vancouver
Juan de Fuca Strait   *Haro Strait*

North Pacific Ocean

Washington

Newport

Oregon

Farallon Islands
Monterey Bay

California

Point Conception

Channel Islands

San Diego

Pacific Coast of North America

Scammon's Lagoon

Vizcaino Peninsula

San Ignacio Lagoon

Baja California

Magdalena Bay

Hawaiian Islands

Lahaina

Revillagigedo Islands

Contents

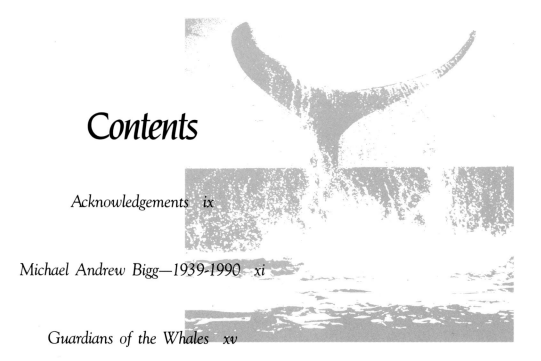

Acknowledgements

Thanks to. . .John and Bev Ford. . .Jane Watson. . .Jim Darling of the West Coast Whale Research Foundation. . .Ken Balcomb of the Centre for Whale Research. . .John Calambokidis of Cascadia Research. . .Steve Swartz and Mary Lou Jones. . .Olga von Ziegesar and Craig Matkin. . .Ian MacAskie. . .Irene and Dave Myers. . .Dr. Ken Langelier of the Island Veterinary Hospital. . .researchers Elley Dorsey, Jonathan Stearn, Rus Hoelzel, Linda Nichol, Pam Stacey, Robin Baird, Dave Bain, and Birgit Kriete. . .ORCALAB's Helena Symonds and Paul Spong. . .Alex and Jarret Morton, for feeding us, for informing us. . .Donna and Bill Mackay, and Anne and Jim Borrowman, for their kind hospitality. . .editor Ian Darragh of Canadian Geographic, for assigning so many whale stories. . .Flip Nicklin, for lending Graeme Ellis a camera. . .Margaret and Patrick Ellis, from whom their son inherited his love and respect for the sea. . .Jason and Dana Ellis, for tolerating such long hours in small boats. . .Janet Barwell-Clarke, Nicole, and Lauren Obee, for their continued tolerance of the grumpy writer downstairs.

Michael Andrew Bigg

1939-1990

The clock of life is wound but once,
And no man has the power
To tell just when the hands will stop
At a late or early hour.
Now is the only time you own,
Live, love, toil with a will,
Place no faith in tomorrow
For the clock may then be still.

—Anonymous

Michael Bigg was gifted with an enviable talent for inspiring others to join in new challenges, to dive headlong into a project and explore it to its full depth. He enkindled a new appreciation of west-coast killer whales and led the scientific community in its quest for knowledge of one of the world's most fascinating creatures.

Though his name is invariably associated with killer whales, Bigg was widely respected for his knowledge of other marine mammals. Before accepting an appointment in 1970 as Canada's head of marine-mammal research in the Pacific, he'd earned a master's degree from the University of B.C. for a study of the population biology of harbour seals. In 1972 he was awarded a Ph.D for his work on the reproductive ecology of harbour seals. As a biologist for the Department of Fisheries and Oceans, Bigg studied fur seals in B.C. and the Pribilof Islands, and maintained a captive colony of fur seals at Nanaimo's Pacific Biological Station. He organized the transplant of Alaskan sea otters to B.C. waters, began long-term studies of sea lions, and was the nation's representative to the North Pacific Fur Seal Commission.

While his work with these animals was impressive, it was mainly killer whales, a species that absorbed the last two decades of his life, that won Michael Bigg international esteem. What began as a government census of west-coast killer whales eventually became the most comprehensive study of any cetacean species in the world.

In the early 1970s, orca research was propelled into a new era when Bigg discovered that individual killer whales can be identified through photographs. The process has become the foundation for orca studies around the world, providing an insight into killer-whale biology which would otherwise be impossible. In papers presented to the International Whaling Commission in 1990, Bigg provided extensive detail from sixteen years of Pacific Northwest field work: live captures, sustainable harvests, social organization and genealogy, longevity, age determinations, reproduction, mortality, racial variations, foraging habits, seasonal movements, and more.

While many considered Michael Bigg the world's foremost authority on killer whales, others questioned his conclusions. They were based entirely on field observations: it was a nonintrusive, creative approach to scientific research which wasn't readily welcomed by those who felt more comfortable with the typical collect-and-dissect methods of the day. Some simply refused to believe anyone could know so much about a single species. He was occasionally scorned for resisting pressure to publish detailed reports of his findings as his research progressed. Bigg countered the criticism, saying it was impossible to understand the life histories of such long-lived animals in just a few years: to produce papers based on incomplete data would be risking the publication of inaccurate detail.

Though he published certain aspects of his research, Bigg's goal was to present the entire Pacific Northwest killer-whale picture, a task which completely consumed him. But in 1984, well over a decade into the work, Bigg was diagnosed with cancer. For six years he endured the treatments, the hopes, and the setbacks of fighting a terminal illness.

At times it seemed he was driven by his disease: he worked furiously, determined to finish writing the report of all he had learned about killer whales. He completed the work, but it seemed a certainty that Bigg, living his last days at his parents' home, would not survive to see his report in print. Graeme Ellis, his closest friend and colleague, called the publisher in England, who received the first copy off the press as they spoke. Through a series of events it was rushed to Canada and delivered to Bigg's parents as an ambulance was taking their son to hospital.

They took the report to him and he was able to see it in print and look through it before he died. It was October 18, 1990.

To see what he considered his life's work in print was an appropriate final reward for a man so devoted, a man who accomplished so much in a career that was only half complete when he died.

"He was just absolutely driven," says John Ford, marine-mammal scientist at the Vancouver Public Aquarium. Ford recalls one incident which typifies Bigg's insatiable thirst for knowledge of Pacific Northwest killer whales. It was a summer day when he and Bigg, in separate boats, were following a pod of whales off the Victoria waterfront. The whales spread out over both sides of the B.C.-Washington border. "It was a frustrating day and Mike, when he's frustrated, there's no stopping him." By late afternoon the whales began to gather in Haro Strait and Bigg decided to spend the night with them, bobbing about in his five-metre skiff. He ran back to Victoria to pick up fuel and some packaged apple pies. Ford went home, leaving Bigg a phone number to call in an emergency.

"So the phone rings about midnight," Ford recalls. "It's Mike and he doesn't know where he is. He's just out in the middle of Georgia Strait somewhere. It got dark and he was having to turn off the engine and listen for blows. He'd hear them in one direction, start the motor, and take off. So when he called on the radio phone he was absolutely lost; the whales were gone, it was pitch black, and the only light he had was the little red LED that lit up on the radio when he held it to transmit. He was actually quite concerned because he had lost his lucky hat."

"What he used for a chart was basically a map of Vancouver Island with Mac Tac all over it so it wouldn't fall apart in the rain and seas. He had it all rolled up in a ball, so to see where you were you had to unravel this ball of Mac Tac," Ford laughs.

Bigg's absent-minded-scientist image revealed itself only occasionally. He was better known for his articulate manner and quick-witted sense of humour. "He was a very likable person," says Ford. "He had incredible integrity and an infectious dedication to the animals, to science, and to the truth."

Bigg held a firm belief that the truth would always be revealed and he often relied on that belief to deal with skepticism of his orca research. Perhaps the same conviction helped him accept the inevitability of his untimely death.

"I'm not afraid of what lies ahead for me," Bigg wrote in an open letter to his friends and family before his death. "The whole process seems so natural when you think about it. We who have spent our lives watching the life cycles of creatures around us have witnessed many times the start and end of lives of many creatures."

Mike Bigg contributed enormously to the study of killer whales on the Pacific coast, but perhaps his greatest legacy is the loyal organization of whale guardians who ensure that his aspirations did not die with him. While many are frustrated by his absence, most admit to a sense of duty to Bigg, even though he can no longer share the excitement of their discoveries. "We still do it for Mike," they say.

Guardians of the Whales

In the early 1970s whales off the Pacific coast of North America were still being killed and dissected for science. Some prominent researchers believed it was impossible to repeatedly observe individual wild whales; our knowledge could be gleaned only by examining a large series of specimens. The newest craze was captive whales and, like the public, scientists were lured to aquariums by the mystique of the largest animals on earth. There was an urgency to their work: no one had practised cetacean husbandry; no one knew how to keep whales alive in tanks.

Meanwhile, another faction of the scientific fraternity was beginning to challenge accepted doctrines. They agreed that dead and captive whales were useful, but disagreed that they provided the only research opportunities. They had learned that whales carry markings as distinctive as human fingerprints. By photographing nicks, scratches, and skin pigmentations, one whale could indeed be distinguished from another. By the mid-1970s thousands of photographs had been amassed; hundreds of whales had been identified—one by one.

Through catalogues of photographed whales, researchers counted the orcas of the Pacific Northwest, traced the seasonal travels of humpback and gray whales, developed new insights into the behaviour and societies of the world's whales. Perfecting identification and study techniques became a worldwide undertaking as their data was shared with researchers throughout the Pacific, the Atlantic, and other oceans.

The revelation that whales can be studied in their own domain opened a new frontier in the field of cetacean research. It was a particularly attractive proposition: scientists accustomed to working around the slimy slipways of whaling stations or the spurious environments of aquariums were suddenly compelled to follow the whales to exotic climes, to spend their field seasons on the sea, discovering the undiscovered.

It was soon apparent that we knew virtually nothing of wild whales. Humpbacks and grays, hunted to the brink of extinction, were slowly recovering, but killer whales,

A HUMPBACK CALF CASTS A WARY EYE TOWARD PHOTOGRAPHER GRAEME ELLIS AS IT RISES FOR A BREATH OF AIR. ELLIS AND HIS YOUNG SON, JASON, FREQUENTLY SWAM WITH HUMPBACK WHALES OFF LAHAINA. ONCE, WHILE CLIMBING INTO THE WATER, ELLIS INADVERTENTLY STEPPED ONTO THE BACK OF A WHALE LYING QUIETLY BENEATH THE BOAT.

for the first time, were being seriously harvested and shipped to aquariums for public display. How many were out there; how many could we take before the "resource" was depleted? How quickly do whales recover from human exploitation? How do our uses and abuses of Pacific fisheries affect the survival of whales? What impacts do our industrial ventures have on the habitats of wild whales?

Photo-identification, a major breakthrough, was only a beginning. We've since learned that orca pods consist of matriarchal groups that stay together for life, but the fathers of animals within the groups are unknown. Scientists have determined that each pod speaks its own dialect, but whether their calls are a form of communication remains a mystery. We know now that there are separate races of orcas on this coast with distinct habits and subtle differences in appearance. Still a great deal remains to be discovered. There is no authenticated report of a person ever seeing killer whales breeding in the wild. No one is sure where orcas travel between sightings. There are similar unknowns with other species: the exact meaning of the famous humpback-whale song has not been determined. And though researchers spend countless hours watching the courtship rituals of humpback whales, apparently no one has witnessed these animals actually mating.

The progression of research through the decades has instilled a greater public sympathy for the plight of the world's whales. With growing knowledge comes an increasing concern, a fonder fascination. Researchers, whether by intention or circumstance, have become unofficial guardians of the whales. Pure, objective wildlife scientists are not afforded the luxury of emotional attachments to their subjects, and many would balk at being labelled "guardians" of a species. Their papers and reports disclose little sentimentality toward the animals which preoccupy their lives. But their stories and conversations disregard the scientific formalities, revealing an inconcealable devotion to the animals, a commitment to the whales' unfettered existence in the wild. Their findings influence the decisions which affect the future of these intriguing leviathans. More often than not, it is these scientific "purists" who are at the forefront of battles over the rights and protection of wild whales.

In all there are nine species of baleen whales in the North Pacific and about thirty types of toothed whales, including porpoises and dolphins. All have received some degree of attention from researchers. Gray whales, humpbacks, and orcas are most often seen in near-shore waters along the Pacific coast and therefore have been studied most extensively. Killer whales have captured the interest of the greatest number of researchers and more is known about these animals than any other cetacean. There are literally hundreds of people researching whales and entire volumes have been written about each of the major species.

It would be nearly impossible, and undoubtedly tedious, to try, in a single book, to cover all of the studies conducted on these animals since the early 1970s. *Guardians of the Whales* is not a textbook, but a story of the adventures, the accomplishments, and philosophies of some of the people involved in the study of our most frequently observed cetaceans. It is meant to inform, to entertain, and to encourage an empathy for free-roaming wild animals. . .animals that we humans almost wiped from the face of the earth.

A HUMPBACK WHALE RAISES ITS FLUKES IN CHOPPY SEAS OFF LAHAINA. THROUGH PHOTO-IDENTIFICATION DR. JIM DARLING (AT THE HELM OF THE BOAT) DISCOVERED THAT HUMPBACKS WINTERING IN HAWAII MAY SPEND THEIR SUMMERS IN ALASKAN WATERS. NOW SOME THIRTY-FIVE HUNDRED HUMP-BACKS HAVE BEEN IDENTIFIED IN THE NORTH PACIFIC.

CHAPTER ONE

Killer Whales

They've come from all directions, these whales, for a few hours' respite from the din of ships and fish boats in Johnstone Strait. All is quiet here as they loll in the afternoon sun, milling about in the shadows of trees above the shore. Black triangular fins slide along the edge of the gravel beach; occasionally a front flipper sluggishly slaps the surface. There is no breaching, no spy-hopping; these orcas are here to rest and mingle with others of their kind.

We keep our distance, drifting in silence, mesmerized by the quiescent scene before us. A dozen have congregated near the beach and at least as many again are moving toward them: a few loners, pairs of cows and calves, groups of three and four. Some pause within touching distance of the boat, turning a curious eye toward the trespassers in their domain. These sensitive cetaceans are acutely in tune with their environment, and our effort to be unobtrusive is futile.

Willowy spouts rise over the western horizon and we count three more killer whales heading toward the beach. Off our stern and starboard side others appear in the distance. In all, about forty-five whales—members of six pods—are within our field of vision. Another three dozen whales from these families are likely nearby, beyond the scope of our binoculars.

BACKLIT BLOWS. WHALES FROM A NUMBER OF PODS TAKE A LEISURELY AFTERNOON SWIM DOWN JOHNSTONE STRAIT. KILLER WHALES FROM SIXTEEN PODS INHABIT THE WATERS OF THIS AREA DURING SUMMER. THEY ARE OCCASIONALLY SIGHTED AT OTHER TIMES OF YEAR.

It's one of those rare late-summer evenings when their underwater acoustical world is untainted by the irritating whir of speedboats or the pulsating drone of diesel engines. With eyes closed I listen through the hydrophone to their dialogue, to the eerie, high-pitched calls and sharp, staccato clicks. I hear them puffing as they break the surface and, without opening my eyes, envision the momentary mist that lingers over their immense bodies before they dive. An eagle screeches in the forest above the whales, perhaps a warning, a signal of its discontent with our intrusion. As we drift on a dead-calm sea, I sense the spiritual eminence these animals hold in the folklore of coastal natives. If ever there was a time and place to believe in magic, surely this is it.

A dense fog bank is rolling down the strait toward us. Ripples fracture the mirrorlike surface and we turn up our collars against the breeze. Wisps of mist creep through the trees: soft and smokelike, it settles in the channels and bays, obscuring rocks and reefs that surround offshore islets. The whales move off in small groups, as they had arrived, and the sound of their intermittent blows fades as they are swallowed by the fog. Soon we too are enveloped. With compass, charts, sounder, and radar, we grope through a maze of reef-ridden waterways to Telegraph Cove.

These channels, between northeast Vancouver Island and mainland British Columbia, are the world's most reliable orca-watching territory. Each summer killer whales funnel down through Queen Charlotte Strait into the constricted waters of Johnstone Strait, running a gauntlet of trollers, gillnetters, seiners, and anglers. Like fishermen, the whales are lured by millions of Pacific salmon returning home to spawn. Sockeye, chum, coho, chinook, and pink salmon fill the bellies of whales and fish boats from late spring to autumn.

Unlike salmon, killer whales on this coast are not plentiful: only four hundred or so regularly patrol the shorelines of northern Washington and British Columbia, and probably a similar number inhabits Alaskan waters. Yet, despite their scarcity, orcas have become a symbol of the Pacific Northwest. Their distinctive black and white bodies appear on the logos of credit unions, publishers, and tourist brochures. They star in television documentaries and videos, and breach month by month through innumerable kitchen calendars. Their flashing flukes embellish magazines, posters, T-shirts, and storybooks, and their images adorn the artistry of modern-day coastal Indians.

Thousands of nature lovers take to the sea each summer in kayaks, cruisers, runabouts, or whale-watching boats to fatten their photo albums with blurry shots of distant dorsal fins and whale spouts. These orcas have been serenaded by flutes and live rock bands, and stalked relentlessly by film crews from England, Japan, France, Australia, and other faraway places. Researchers eavesdrop on their subaqueous conversations, and photograph

A YOUNG RESIDENT KILLER WHALE COMES TO RUB ON THE GRAVEL SEAFLOOR AT ROBSON BIGHT (MICHAEL BIGG) ECOLOGICAL RESERVE, ONE OF THE FEW PLACES IN THE WORLD WHERE ORCAS ARE KNOWN TO INDULGE IN THIS BEHAVIOUR. DURING SUMMER, 90 PERCENT OF THE RESIDENT ORCAS THAT FREQUENT JOHNSTONE STRAIT COME TO RUB AT ROBSON BIGHT.

them—one by one—to be catalogued in a genealogical registry of northwest killer whales. You can walk into a library or bookstore and contemplate the family tree of every orca that frequents these near-shore waters. Every whale has an official name—A5, A6, H8, L44, and so on. They have nicknames like Charlie Chin, Top Notch, Tahoma, Merlin, Oreo, or Slick. You can even "adopt" a wild orca by sending a tax-deductible donation to a public aquarium or whale museum. As research subjects, these animals have been studied, followed, and photographed more than any other whales in the world. You can't be a Pacific Northwest killer whale without everybody knowing your business.

Orcamania is a recent phenomenon. It represents a complete about-face in public sentiment toward a species that has suffered more than its share of indignities at the hands of humans. On the coast of North America orcas have been targets for practising air-force bombers; they have been riddled with bullets by vandals and fishermen; they have been dumped in plastic pools to entice buyers to boat shows; their close-knit pods have been disunited by profit-minded aquarium owners.

No one could get away with this now. But as recently as the 1960s and early '70s, the myths and misconceptions that surrounded the killer whale were yet to be unravelled. They were bloodthirsty oceanic predators, and like terrestrial predators, their disfavour was born through our ignorance.

As a youngster on southern Vancouver Island I didn't question the killer whale's unattested infamy. While their arrival in our bay was viewed with mixed feelings, they were undeniable cause for excitement. A whole squadron would glide in from Juan de Fuca Strait, their ominous dagger-shaped dorsal fins slicing the sea like periscopes. With pockets full of rocks we'd clamber up the headlands and scan the seaward edge of the bay, watching, listening for that unmistakable gush of air exploding from their lungs. Any that surfaced within firing range were met by a volley of stones from our slingshots.

These were dangerous beasts. They could smash our rowboats to smithereens and swallow children like us in a single gulp. *Orcinus orca*—the notorious "blackfish"—had no business in our bay, imperilling our safety, and our mothers would lock away the oars and life jackets until they were gone. We resented them for their reputation—though no one had ever been attacked by killer whales—yet we respected them for the awesome fear they instilled in our adolescent hearts.

A PLAYFUL WHALE SOMERSAULTS BENEATH THE MOUNTAINS OF PRINCE WILLIAM SOUND. NOTE THE VISIBLE BLOOD VESSELS ON THE UNDERSIDE OF THE FLUKES.

A CARVING OF A KILLER-WHALE HEAD ON A TOTEM AT ACOUS PENINSULA, NEAR VANCOUVER ISLAND'S CHECLESET BAY. KILLER WHALES ARE A PROMINENT SYMBOL IN THE MYTHOLOGY OF NORTHWEST COAST NATIVES.

Although they'd never been studied, killer whales had been denigrated carnivores for at least a century. "Indeed they may be regarded as marine beasts, that roam over every ocean; entering bays and lagoons, where they spread terror and death among the mammoth balaenas and the smaller species of dolphins," whaling captain Charles Scammon wrote in 1874.

In his book, *The Marine Mammals of the Northwestern Coast of North America*, Scammon's graphic portrayal of the killer whale's hunting prowess is liberally spiced with his personal bias. "Three or four of these voracious animals do not hesitate to grapple with the largest baleen whales; and it is surprising to see those leviathans of the deep so completely paralyzed by the presence of their natural, although diminutive, enemies. Frequently the terrified animal—comparatively of enormous size and superior strength—evinces no effort to escape, but lies in a helpless condition, or makes but little resistance to the assaults of its merciless destroyers. The attack of these wolves of the ocean upon their gigantic prey may be likened, in some respects, to a pack of hounds holding the stricken deer at bay. They cluster about the animal's head, some of their number breaching over it, while others seize it by the lips and haul the bleeding monster under water; and when captured, should the mouth be open, they eat out its tongue. . . . In whatever quarter of the world the Orcas are found, they seem always intent upon seeking something to destroy or devour."

This perspective prevailed well into the middle of the next century. In a book entitled *Killer Whale!*, published in 1963, authors Joseph J. Cook and William L. Wisner open with these words: "The fiercest, most terrifying animal in all the world lives in the sea, not on land. . . . Lions, tigers and great bears are considered savage animals, but many times more powerful and far more vicious than any of these is the killer whale."

With its "vicious instincts," they say, "orcas are capable of attacking anything that swims, no matter how large. They are afraid of nothing, not even boats or ships."

"The killer whale is well designed for a career of destruction and mayhem," the book continues. "Its jaws and their terrible teeth are a kind of animated chopping machine which can tear great chunks from a giant sea animal and bite a large fish in half."

The largest member of the dolphin family, the killer whale is radically dissimilar from other species of the same family, Cook and Wisner claim. "How different the orca, which seems to be filled with a burning hatred! Nothing that lives or moves in or on the water is safe from its assaults. Its size, power, speed, agility and disposition have made this black monster greatly feared wherever it is known."

Perhaps these authors used the same research sources as the U.S. Navy. A publication by the navy's Hydrographic Office at the time warned that killer whales "will attack human beings at every opportunity."

North of the border the Canadian Department of Fisheries and Oceans also espoused the myth, installing a machine-gun mount at Seymour Narrows, south of Johnstone Strait,

TWO MEMBERS OF B POD SCAN THEIR TERRESTRIAL SURROUNDINGS BY SPY-HOPPING NEAR ROBSON BIGHT.

to dissuade whales from swimming toward the Vancouver Island town of Campbell River. Fishermen and resort owners there had complained that killer whales were ruining the fishing in Discovery Passage, between Seymour Narrows and Georgia Strait.

Ideas for solutions were solicited from fisheries officers along the B.C. coast who, in 1958, provided a wide range of comments. "The only effective means of taking the blackfish would appear to be a fast maneuverable boat, possibly along the lines of a crash boat, equipped with a harpoon gun. . . . A suitable gun should be chosen for the job, particularly a small Bazooka type with an explosive bullet. . . . A herd should be followed in open water by a suitable boat with the proper equipment in an attempt to destroy as many as possible."

One officer recommended trolling a baited line to entice a whale close enough to strike it with a harpoon attached to a buoy. "If one of these whales was put in difficulties by having a harpoon and buoy line attached to him there would seem little doubt that the cannibalistic traits of the rest of the shoal, if left alone, would soon put the finishing touches on him."

The minutes from a 1960 meeting in Campbell River, in retrospect, are equally entertaining. "Mr. Pike thought it would be possible for a number of boats to head blackfish into shallow water where they would either beach themselves or could be dynamited. . . . If the Air Force was to drop half a dozen bombs on them none would be seen in the Narrows for six months."

Eventually the recommended "control measures" included "the use of a machine gun, depth charges, fragmentation bombs, dynamite and mortars." This weaponry never was used, and though the machine gun mount was installed at Seymour Narrows, the gun never was fired. Shooting at killer whales from fish boats, however, remained an acceptable pastime: one-quarter of the orcas caught for aquariums in the 1960s and '70s bore bullet wounds.

The first inkling that the killer whale's ignoble image was misconceived arose in 1964 under bizarre circumstances. The orca, in spite of its nefariousness, was considered symbolic of Pacific Northwest waters. But it was thought to be too dangerous to exhibit live, so the Vancouver Public Aquarium hired a sculptor to harpoon a whale and use the carcass as the basis of a model for public display. After a lengthy vigil a young orca was harpooned off Saturna Island, in B.C.'s southern Gulf Islands. Moby Doll, as the unfortunate whale came to be known, refused to succumb to the wound, so was dragged across Georgia Strait and housed in a pen at Vancouver Harbour. Though curious, the public seemed largely indifferent to the plight of Moby Doll: it was, after all, an era when governments condoned the shooting of killer whales.

ORCAS TOUR THE GLASS-CALM WATERS OF PRINCE WILLIAM SOUND. RESEARCHERS WHO HAVE STUDIED ALASKAN ORCAS SINCE THE EARLY 1980S ESTIMATE THAT MORE THAN TWO HUNDRED TRAVEL IN PRINCE WILLIAM SOUND.

The world's first captive killer whale, surprisingly, was not the pernicious predator people expected. It was docile, even friendly, and soon researchers from across the continent were coming to visit Moby Doll. Among them was Michael Bigg, a twenty-five-year-old biology student who eventually became the world's foremost authority on *Orcinus orca.* Moby Doll, which later was found to be a male, won international acclaim before it died of internal mycotic infections, eighty-six days after its dubious abduction. During its short-lived incarceration, the young whale gave scientists their first close look at a living member of its species. Recordings of its underwater vocalizations provided evidence that killer whales use echolocation.

The Moby-Doll experience piqued the interest of enterprising businessmen who envisioned an applauding public enthralled by the tricks of well-trained captive killer whales. Before Moby Doll's untimely demise, there had been two efforts to capture live orcas. One netted off southern California in 1961, by Marineland of the Pacific, died within two days. Captors for Marineland botched another attempt the next year off Bellingham, Washington. They lassoed a female and the rope became wrapped around the propeller. The whale and an accompanying bull reportedly charged the boat: the female was shot to death and the bull quickly vanished.

The entrepreneurial spirit wasn't confined to businessmen. Eight months after Moby Doll's death, two fishermen accidentally snared two orcas, a bull and a calf, in a gill net near Namu, an isolated cannery town ninety kilometres north of Vancouver Island. While one fisherman was preparing to free the whales, the sound of cash registers was ringing in the ears of the other: he offered the pair of "blackfish" to the first person who could come up with quick, and adequate, cash. The calf escaped, and soon after, Ted Griffin, owner of the Seattle Public Aquarium, arrived with $8,000 for the bull. Namu, the whale that became instant international news, was towed 700 kilometres to Seattle in a makeshift floating pen. During the journey a group of thirty or forty whales overtook Griffin's flotilla and followed it for several hours. A cow and two calves, probably the immediate family, stayed with Namu for 240 kilometres.

On July 28, 1965, one month to the day after closing the sale, Griffin's whale floated into Seattle's Pier 56 to a cheering crowd and a Dixieland band. Five thousand paying spectators came to see Namu at the aquarium on the first day. Griffin, who admits it was "almost a ruling passion" to own his own killer whale, was swimming with his prized pet before the end of the next month. Within two months of its arrival, 120,000 people had paraded past America's first captive orca. Griffin had gambled $60,000 to bring the animal before the masses. One year later, Namu was dead.

But the freshly sown seeds of a northwest whale-catching industry were alive and germinating. Griffin teamed up with Don Goldsberry, a collector from the Point Defiance Aquarium in Tacoma, Washington, to capture killer whales in seine nets and ship them to oceanariums around the world. Among them was Skana, the first orca to live in a Canadian oceanarium, purchased for $25,000 in 1967 by the Vancouver Aquarium. After a publicity stint at a boat show, she was delivered to the aquarium, her home for thirteen years. With killer whales fetching $20,000 or more apiece, Griffin, Goldsberry, and other commercial "whalers" were scrambling to satisfy aquariums in Canada, the United States, Japan, Europe, and Australia. By 1975 more than fifty orcas from B.C. and Washington waters were permanently ensconced in oceanariums. Another dozen had died during capture operations.

At first there was little opposition to the captures. Killer whales, to many, were vermin, and besides, there were probably thousands out there: to take a few for the amusement—and education—of millions of people was a small sacrifice.

* * *

In those days, Graeme Ellis, a curly-haired kid from Campbell River, could bonk a killer whale with a rock at thirty yards. "It was the thing to do in those days. We didn't even conceive of killer whales being anything but a threat." As a teenager his views began to change. He'd read about Moby Doll, the gentle killer that accepted food from human hands. His sympathies were further aroused when he saw his first captive orca. "Skana was stuck in a little tank at the Vancouver boat show. It was pretty awful. I remember being disgusted."

A year later Ellis, eighteen and fresh out of high school, was given a job that launched him into a whale-research career that has since absorbed his life. His father was an Anglican minister involved with the Columbia Coast Mission, which had waterfront land at Pender Harbour, on the mainland side of Georgia Strait. The Vancouver Aquarium had made arrangements to keep recently caught whales at the Pender Harbour property, and Ellis was hired to feed them. Marineland of the Pacific had already collected two whales; two pregnant cows were awaiting shipment to Marine World Africa U.S.A., and a male calf named Hyak was headed for Vancouver. Of the remaining three, one died and the two survivors, both bulls, became Ellis's wards.

The whales were held in separate pens and Ellis devoted much of his time to Skookum Cecil, the larger bull, because he wouldn't eat. Ellis soon became adept at scuttling along slippery logs, bucket of herring in hand, under the watchful eyes of a hungry orca. "I was nervous for sure," Ellis recalls, "a big animal swimming along right beside me. I thought of the reputation killer whales had in those days."

After a month of whistling at the whale, calling and coaxing, the big bull still refused

Ellis's offers of dead fish. Then one day Ellis was splashing water on the whale when it splashed back—the first response to Ellis's tireless efforts. Skookum Cecil's appetite picked up and the whale came to enjoy being scratched and rubbed by its feeder.

It was time, Ellis thought bravely, to swim with this animal. He'd read of Ted Griffin's amicable relationship with Namu and their hours of swimming together at the Seattle Aquarium. Was that normal, or exceptional?

Clad in wet suit, mask, and snorkel, a jittery Ellis slipped alone into the pen with a four-tonne killer whale. "I put my head underwater and he came at me; you could see him coming through the murk there, and he opened his jaws as he came towards me. I just went out of the water like a shot," Ellis says, chuckling at the memory. "He scared the hell out of me. One moment I was in the water, the next moment I was standing on the logs.

"Then I thought, for some reason, that it was a bluff. I had to try it again. So I went in and he did the same thing, came around and opened his mouth up, then snapped it shut. I stayed there and he came up, like a dog, and sort of rubbed up against me. I scratched him down the side and he did it again. He changed completely when I didn't get out of the water. I was still scared, but felt confident he wasn't going to hurt me."

Ellis's friendship with Skookum Cecil, however, was short-lived. On an early August morning, four months after the whale's capture, Ellis wandered down to the pen just in time to see the big bull blow once, dive, and head out to sea. A heavy cluster of mussels had torn open a side of the pen's netting, leaving an opening for Skookum Cecil's hasty exit. They chased him for a week without success.

So Ellis lived alone through the next winter with the one remaining whale. "It was wonderful to work with the animal. I basically lived with him. Every day I went down and played with him all day. Just one animal in a pen and myself living in a cabin right above it. That was my occupation."

But his occupation, like his friendship with Skookum Cecil, was short-lived. The aquarium summoned Ellis to Vancouver to tell him his job was being chopped with other cutbacks. Ellis, who had developed "an incredible bond" with the animal, was shocked. To add insult to injury, he later received a call from the aquarium informing him that someone had released the whale. "I still have no idea who it was, but of course the aquarium must have thought I'd made a phone call and said to let him go." The whale never was seen again.

At that time Bob Wright was opening Sealand of the Pacific in Victoria, B.C. Fortunately for Ellis, the world was not rife with whale trainers and he easily landed a job at the new aquarium. Wright had acquired Haida, a young bull, one of five killer

whales taken by Griffin and Goldsberry in October of 1968. Ellis, always eager to share a whale's water, soon learned in whose territory he was swimming. Haida was swirling around the pool, with Ellis clinging to the dorsal fin, when the whale tilted its passenger toward the deck, trying to drop him onto a platform. Ellis didn't take the hint. Haida made a second attempt, dumping his trainer at the edge of the pool and momentarily holding him underwater. Ellis, frightened half to death, grabbed a chain dangling from the platform and hung on.

"He was looking at me really close; his eye was almost right up to my face, with his nose on my shoulder and he held me there. He just pushed me right down. I was really scared. I was hanging on to that chain for dear life. I thought he was going to drown me, stuff me under the side of the pool, but he just held me there for a few seconds. He lifted his head off and looked at me. I said, 'Okay,' and climbed out of the pool.

"No problem after that; I swam with him lots of times, but as soon as I got the warning that he'd had enough I got out of the pool. I just became more sensitive to his

warnings. You really have to watch for that. I've seen it lots of times, watching killer-whale shows. You can tell when the whale's agitated and doesn't want to be doing what he's being asked to do."

While employed by Sealand, Ellis, more by default than desire, joined the growing fraternity of whale catchers. Wright's team was scouting for whales off the Victoria waterfront on a blustery winter day in 1970. Something flashed in the afternoon sun and Wright spotted whale spouts between the waves. Suddenly a white whale—an extraordinarily rare animal—breached in the midst of four other killer whales.

Everyone jumped into action. The whales appeared headed for Pedder Bay, where a boat and gill net were ready. Through the day they watched anxiously until shortly after sundown, when all five orcas casually swam into the bay. The net was stretched across the entrance, corralling the whales. An exuberant Ellis and his teammates stood watch through the night, coming down from the high that had held them through the afternoon and evening. By morning, with the excitement of the catch behind him, Ellis had had sufficient time to search his soul.

"I just turned sick. It was a real challenge—you don't think you're really going to catch a whale. But once it happened, I began to wonder: do we really need them? What are we going to do with them now? I wanted to let them go."

Repeated attempts to feed the orcas failed. Salmon, herring, ling: the whales would have none. Within four weeks of the capture, two cows, Chimo the white whale and Nootka, were moved to Sealand. Haida, who hadn't seen another of his species for six months, was segregated from the newcomers by a net. Initially Haida was disinterested, relating more to his trainer than to Chimo and Nootka. When the new whales refused to eat, Haida eventually picked up a herring and pushed it through the net. Soon the whales were feeding on dead fish, regaining their strength.

It wasn't until several years later that researchers discovered there were two races of killer whales off the Pacific Northwest coast. So-called "resident" whales, which are seen frequently near shore in summer, feed on fish. "Transients," which roam farther afield, eat seals, sea lions, porpoises, and larger whales. Haida was a fish-eating resident. Those captured at Pedder Bay were transients: Chimo and Nootka had probably never eaten fish until they were encaged with Haida, unable to catch their own food.

There were similar problems with the three whales at Pedder Bay. During the tenth week one died and was quietly towed out to sea under cover of darkness. The next week, listless and emaciated, the two survivors began to accept dead salmon. Both whales, a cow and a large bull known as Charlie Chin because of its protruding lower jaw, were destined for an aquarium in Texas.

A STREAM OF BUBBLES TRAILS A KILLER WHALE AS IT EXHALES JUST BELOW THE SURFACE. ORCAS TRAVELLING AT HIGH SPEED OFTEN BLOW UNDERWATER BEFORE TAKING A SPLIT-SECOND BREATH AT THE SURFACE AND DIVING BACK DOWN.

By then Ellis had seen enough of the captive-whale trade. "I was obviously a naive kid, nineteen years old and I didn't understand business, but I got really disillusioned. The whole thing was money-oriented: you sell the whales, you sell the shows, and if the whales don't perform, people don't want to see them. As a trainer I had people demand their money back because a whale wouldn't jump if it was off its show. I got quite cynical about the reasons the public was there."

The Sealand performances were less humiliating than the spectacles staged at American oceanariums. Whales in hats and sunglasses had their teeth scrubbed by pretty girls with giant brushes. Trainers, like broncobusting cowboys, rode the whales around the pool. They porpoised through hoops, jumped for beach balls, sang on cue, and saturated awestruck audiences.

"Those shows made me want to puke," says Ellis. "It was degrading to the animal. I felt like they were displaying the trainers, not the animals. That's probably when I really tipped over. I just thought it was sick."

So the naive, disillusioned whale trainer boarded a boat and set sail for Mexico. While he was gone, someone sneaked across the darkened waters of Pedder Bay and set the whales free. Charlie Chin and his companion had been immured for seven months. They've since been seen roaming the seas between northern Washington and southeast Alaska. It appears the cow has produced at least three calves since her return to the wild.

* * *

While Ellis was regrouping in the tropics, Paul Spong was starting his observations of wild orcas in Blackfish Sound. It was 1970, Spong's first year on isolated Hanson Island, two kilometres across Johnstone Strait from northeast Vancouver Island. More than two decades later Spong is still there, with his partner, Helena Symonds, and their daughter, Anna, running a research station called ORCALAB.

After leaving his native New Zealand, Spong earned a Ph.D. in psychology at the University of California, then accepted an assistant professorship at the University of British Columbia. Half of his salary was paid by the Vancouver Aquarium, where he studied sensory perception of captive orcas.

He worked closely with Skana for two years, developing an intimate friendship. In 1969 a newspaper covered a lecture given by Spong in which he suggested that Skana would prefer freedom over confinement. The Vancouver Aquarium was less than pleased: though captive orcas were still new, the first hints of opposition were beginning to emerge. Spong's research with Skana came to an abrupt halt.

"While he was considered something of a renegade in local academic circles, he was a bit of a legend among eco-freaks on the West Coast, having been fired from the aquarium for daring to state in public that the whale he had been studying—named Skana—wanted to be free," writes Bob Hunter of Greenpeace. "Having been kicked out on the street for that radical statement he had moved to Hanson Island—not far from the Kwakiutl Indian village of Alert Bay—where he had set up a whale-watching station, swimming among the great toothed whales, playing music to them, and coming eventually to the conclusion that their intelligence, while of a different order than ours, was far greater than anyone was willing to believe," Hunter says in his book, *Warriors of the Rainbow.* "Spong wanted Greenpeace to use such clout as it had to join him in his campaign to end the mass killing of whales. It was a notion that was still ahead of its time, even among Greenpeacers."

Some of Spong's other notions were ahead of their time, and his early antics at Hanson Island—playing his flute while floating in a kayak among wild killer whales—earned him a reputation as an oddball. When he brought in a floating rock band to entertain the whales, the locals were convinced he was crazy.

Spong believed through his aquarium research that orcas, being highly acoustic animals, were fond of music, particularly live music, which has a greater fidelity than recordings. Hyak, Skana's companion, fancied violins and classical Indian pieces, and Spong often invited flautists, guitarists, and other musicians to the aquarium to play for the whales.

"Hyak would cozy right up to it," says Spong. "He'd sit there so the point of his head was just millimetres from the strings of the guitar. He'd be listening away as if he was in ecstasy." Aquarium Director Dr. Murray Newman couldn't be persuaded to bring in a chamber orchestra for the whales: some twenty years later, with Newman still in charge, the Vancouver Symphony staged a performance on the deck of the whale pool.

Spong tried to introduce musical culture to wild-orca society by projecting euphonious sounds into the water, but could arouse no interest. Something more sensational was needed, so the rock band Fireweed set up aboard a boat and, with power supplied through a cord from shore, blasted some tunes across the waters of Blackfish Sound. A few inquisitive whales approached the boat, slowly swam around it and left, a somewhat

disappointing response. "But it was great entertainment for us," Spong smiles.

A second oceangoing recital drew a more gratifying reaction. Fireweed had finished a gig in Alert Bay, on Cormorant Island, not far from ORCALAB. They piled aboard the *D'Sonoqua*, a yet-to-be-rigged ferro-cement sailboat, plugged their gear into the vessel's power, and boogied down the strait toward Hanson Island. Soon a pod of orcas arrived to investigate the commotion.

The whales, about twenty of them, lined up abreast behind the boat and swam slowly along the surface as the boat cruised across the sea, the band blaring from the decks. "It was really great," Spong laughs, thinking back twenty years. "The local fishermen thought we were nuts."

Spong held his position at UBC until 1972, coming each summer to Hanson Island, where he set up a network of hydrophones to monitor the movements of whales. ORCALAB, at the northeastern end of the island, sits at a crossroads for travelling whales. Orcas from Johnstone, Queen Charlotte, and Broughton straits travel the waters that surround Hanson Island—Blackfish Sound on the north, Blackney Passage on the east, Weynton Passage on the west, and Johnstone Strait on the south.

A simple explanation for the movements of orcas around Hanson Island is fish: where fish are abundant, there are orcas. But Helena Symonds, who joined Spong at ORCALAB in 1979, believes the explanation is not so rudimentary. "It is a reliable fishing area, but we think it's more significant for other reasons: it seems to be a meeting place also. Social reasons."

The World-War-Two-vintage hydrophones, and reports from travelling mariners, allow ORCALAB to track the whales without chasing them in boats. When whales come within hydrophone range, Symonds plots their travels on a map. Many whales consistently vocalize at specific points, she says. For example, as they round Cracroft Point, southwest of Blackfish Sound, they usually announce their arrival. Some whales appear to run an "escort service," leaving an area to meet another pod, then returning with the new pod. "There are whales breaching and spy-hopping; they're vocal, excited, when these new groups come in. The networking and the hydrophone array all start to give us this much more in-depth picture."

Spong, who refuses to call orcas "killer whales," had recognized the complexity and sociability of the species during the early days of his career, even though little study had been done. He also recognized a need to end the destruction of orcas and other whales. He became a Canadian director of Project Jonah, launched in California in 1972 to tell the world about the plight of the earth's whales. In the early seventies he managed to convince Greenpeace to branch away from nuclear-weapons protests and add whales to their causes. While Greenpeace was confronting Russian whalers on the high seas, Spong was in England feeding reports and photographs of the confrontations to a meeting of the International Whaling Commission.

Then, armed with slides, projectors, and mounds of whale information, Spong travelled to Japan to stage the "Greenpeace Whale Show." He made nineteen appearances, all covered by newspapers, magazines, and national television, reaching a total of thirty million Japanese.

He also distributed a poster of a killer whale breaching in a sunset, a vivid portrayal of free-roaming cetaceans. Ironically, the image was of Charlie Chin, the whale that had escaped in 1970, with help from an unknown accomplice, from the pen at Pedder Bay. "Wherever that particular photo appeared," writes Bob Hunter, "you knew that Paul Spong had been there at some point in the previous few years, as he had wound his way around the world, turning people on to the whales."

* * *

While Spong was crusading to save the whales, a ground swell of opposition to catching orcas for aquariums was brewing along the B.C. and Washington coasts. By 1970 three dozen had been taken from these waters and permits for more were outstanding. Though no one had counted, it was still assumed there were thousands out there.

In keeping with traditional wildlife-management practices, the Canadian government determined that a census should be conducted if we were to continue "harvesting" wild orcas. Only in recent years, with a few exceptions, have North American governments funded significant research on unharvestable animals. Whether it's waterfowl, fish, carnivores, ungulates, or marine mammals, the rule of thumb has been to spend money on our publicly owned wild animals only if we plan to kill them, or if they harm other species we'd like to kill. In the case of wild orcas, the effects of catching them for aquariums differs little from killing them: they are gone either way.

So Dr. Michael Bigg, who in 1970 became Canada's head of marine-mammal research on the west coast, was instructed to carry out a killer-whale census. Bigg, who'd earned his degrees studying harbour seals, dived into the project with characteristic zeal. He sent

DR. PAUL SPONG OF ORCALAB LISTENS TO HIS NETWORK OF HYDROPHONES IN THE BLACK-FISH SOUND AREA. SPONG HAS BEEN MONITORING THE MOVE-MENTS OF ORCAS THROUGH THEIR UNDERWATER VOCALIZA-TIONS SINCE 1970. (BRUCE OBEE PHOTO)

out fifteen thousand questionnaires to lightkeepers, ferry operators, fishermen, and others who travelled and lived along the coast. He asked them to record killer-whale sightings on one day, July 27, 1971. Five hundred responded and the results were disturbing, even shocking: we didn't have thousands of orcas; we had 350 at best.

Similar counts in the next two years verified the numbers. During the second year Bigg's team cruised Johnstone Strait, where most whales had been counted, to observe their behaviour. They took pictures along the way, including one of a whale—later known as Stubbs—with a severely injured dorsal fin, perhaps from a collision with a boat propeller.

"A photograph of the mutilated dorsal fin taken in 1972 led to the detailed examination of other fins and the revelation that most showed some degree of injury," says a report by Ian MacAskie, a researcher who worked closely with Bigg. "It was realized that if these marks were long-lasting (as in fact they are), they could be used for individual identification."

They returned to Johnstone Strait in August 1973, "for an intensive study which quickly confirmed that several animals were indeed familiar." They discovered that pigmentation of the white saddle patches varied; there were scars on the skin, scratches and nicks in the dorsal fins.

Bigg and MacAskie had broken new ground. Every whale carried visible markings as distinctive as human fingerprints. If they could identify them one by one, the research possibilities were limitless: abundance, migrations, social hierarchies, population dynamics. Bigg, afflicted by a true scientist's insatiable curiosity, had flipped the lid off a new can of worms.

Graeme Ellis, back from his south-sea sabbatical, was hired in 1973 to scout around for killer whales in winter whenever someone from Bigg's expanding league of volunteers reported a sighting. Together Bigg, MacAskie, and Ellis developed photo-identification methods, consistently shooting each whale from the left side. Inspired by Mike Bigg's contagious enthusiasm, about two hundred unpaid assistants flooded his office with photographs and reports of west-coast orcas.

In the summer of 1974, boats were deployed along the inside waters from southern Vancouver Island to Johnstone Strait to photograph orcas. The next year, when the census area was extended beyond Vancouver Island to Bella Bella, killer whales were photographed along a 575-kilometre stretch of convoluted coast. Thousands of black-and-white pictures were examined under microscopes. It was becoming evident that killer whales didn't swim in schools like fish, but in close-knit family groups, or pods, with a social organization unlike any other in the mammal world. The same animals were seen repeatedly, always with the same companions. Alphanumeric names were assigned to each whale, signifying both its individuality and its pod.

THE TALL, STRAIGHT DORSAL FIN OF AN ORCA HAS NO BONES; IT CONSISTS OF TISSUE AND CARTILAGE. THE VASCULAR SYSTEM IN THE DORSAL FIN HELPS THE WHALE REGULATE ITS BODY TEMPERATURE. THE OPEN BLOWHOLE OF THIS WHALE IS ABOUT AS WIDE AS A HUMAN FIST.

"It was also becoming clear that the pods were members of two separate communities with a dividing line in northern Georgia Strait," says MacAskie's report. "The range of the southern community encompassed Juan de Fuca Strait, Puget Sound and Georgia Strait, while the range of the northern community extended north from Campbell River. Pods within these two communities were judged as northern or southern 'residents' as opposed to a third community classified as 'transients' that differs in several respects. These travel throughout the coastal waters from Washington state to southeast Alaska, and are seldom encountered. While residents feed on fish, transients seem to seek out mammals as their main prey and are probably a separate race of killer whale."

The expanded coverage and individual identities didn't change the numbers; they substantiated them—there was little question that these waters were inhabited by fewer than 350 killer whales.

Bigg delivered his report in 1976, with a recommendation that no orcas be taken from Canada's Pacific waters except to replace those that died in Canadian aquariums. That same year the U.S. National Marine Fisheries Service asked American researcher Ken Balcomb to conduct an orca census in Washington's inside waters. His examination of the so-called southern community corroborated Bigg's findings.

No whales were captured from Washington or B.C. waters after 1976, with the exception of a young whale named Miracle, found in 1977 off the east coast of Vancouver Island, suffering from starvation and bullet wounds. She was rescued from certain death by Sealand of the Pacific in Victoria, where she drowned four years later while trying to escape through a hole in her pen. When captures were restricted in the mid-seventies, more than half the killer whales caught in the northwest for aquariums were already dead.

By that time Iceland, anxious to rid its seas of the loathsome killer whale, had been discovered as a ready source of aquarium orcas. Canada continued to issue permits to replace captive whales as late as 1983, but none was exercised— purchasing orcas from Iceland created less controversy. "One can only speculate on what sort of response an application would receive now, but for killer whales it seems unlikely that one would be approved," Arctic Fisheries Director Gerald Yaremchuk, Canada's spokesman on marine-mammal issues, said in 1991.

After the completion of Bigg's report, federal funding for killer-whale research was cut off. There were no plans to harvest whales; orcas posed little threat to commercial fisheries. Canada's killer-whale case was closed.

Bigg and his colleagues disagreed. In just a few years they'd come to know more than three hundred individual whales. They'd followed them up and down the coast; they'd amassed thousands of ID photographs; they were in the process of naming the whales,

WOLVES OF THE SEA. A PACK OF TRANSIENT KILLER WHALES IN BLACKFISH SOUND ATTACK A STELLER'S SEA LION WEIGHING ABOUT 350 KILOGRAMS. IT IS COMMON FOR TRANSIENT ORCAS TO TOSS ABOUT THEIR PREY BE-FORE KILLING AND EATING IT. THESE WHALES BATTERED THEIR HAPLESS VICTIM FOR TWO HOURS BEFORE DRAGGING IT UNDERWATER BY ITS BACK FLIP-PERS AND DROWNING IT.

and had begun to untangle the intricacies of orca society. A battery of volunteer research assistants was in place, yet the research, so far, was a mere scratch on the surface. There were still many questions. Where do these animals go in winter? Do pods interbreed? Are transients outcasts from resident families? How long do orcas live? What is the meaning of their vocalizations? Are there others out there, perhaps far offshore?

But the most important breakthrough had already been made. Bigg had proven that whale research need not be confined to captive orcas or to the examination of dissected carcasses on the blood-stained slipways of whaling stations. They could be studied, alive and well, in their own realm, an idea considered outlandish only a few years earlier. It was a new frontier in whale research and soon Bigg's pioneering in the identification of killer whales was adapted to other species.

Bigg, with or without the blessing of his employer, wasn't about to quit. As a scientist he was drawn by anticipation, by the persistent urge to unearth the unknown. As a human being he was captivated, like the native Indians of this coast, by the magic of the orcas.

His killer-whale work became his passion, an obsession which earned him international acclaim. Bigg's quest for knowledge of wild orcas was relentless. While studying seals, sea lions, or other species in the field he disregarded departmental memos ordering him to forget about whales. When he encountered whales he followed them, photographed them, and took copious notes of his observations. He travelled the coast on his own time, soliciting help from anyone and everyone with his infectious fervour. He'd think nothing of asking a floatplane pilot to land beside a sport fisherman, then persuade the fisherman to run him over to a nearby pod of whales and click pictures for the rest of the day. Clad in a summer windbreaker, he'd dash off alone in an open speedboat in winter, packing a camera and an Oh Henry bar, and return after dark, oblivious to the hunger pangs in his stomach and the near-hypothermic state of his body. Sighting reports, photographs, and orca stories poured into his office, where he returned every night, every weekend to sort through the endless accumulation of data, information that he willingly shared with all who expressed a legitimate interest.

When Bigg died of cancer in 1990, at the age of 51, he was unquestionably the world's foremost authority on *Orcinus orca.* It wasn't until after his death that his employer recognized the significance of Mike Bigg's killer-whale work: as the 1990s began, the Department of Fisheries and Oceans decided to provide funding for west-coast whale research.

* * *

The census indicated that killer whales were long-lived animals which could be understood only by long-term monitoring. With the help of students, volunteers, and shoestring funding, Bigg, Graeme Ellis, and others managed to spend at least a few weeks each summer, often during their holidays, identifying whales. Initially the most important task was to sort out the who's-who of northwest orcas by identifying each whale and each pod. Documenting births, deaths, and other changes could then be an ongoing process. When it was decided "the study," as it's known in orca circles, would continue indefinitely, they had already determined there were two "resident" communities— southern and northern—as well as an elusive group they called "transients."

Naming the whales and pods at the outset of the study proved more difficult than anticipated. The plan was to name each pod by a letter of the alphabet—A, B, C, etc.— then give a number to each whale and combine it with the pod letter— A1, A2, B1, B2, and so on. Simple in theory; not so simple in practice.

"The first whale recognized was called A1, and because she was so well marked her pod was called A1 pod," says a catalogue of orcas identified by Bigg and his colleagues. "As chance would have it, our first encounters with her pod actually consisted of three pods which just happened to be travelling together. We erroneously considered all of the whales to be members of her pod. When we later discovered our error, it was too late to change the names of the whales in the other two pods. We simply split A1's group into three pods and called each new pod after the most distinctive individual in it. The resultant pods were A1, A4, and A5. Each member in the three pods has the prefix A in its name." A1, the whale, now is dead, but A1, the pod, lives on.

As the study developed, Bigg's crew concentrated on the resident pods of the northern community. Although these whales roam as far as southeast Alaska, they almost invariably appear, along with the salmon, in Queen Charlotte and Johnstone straits sometime in summer. They confined their work to these waters, keeping the survey area to a manageable size. Assisted by anchored and portable hydrophones, radio reports from other boaters, and sightings from lightkeepers, they searched the seas in small boats.

Meanwhile, Ken Balcomb, director of the Centre for Whale Research on Washington's San Juan Island, continued to monitor the southern community. These whales forage from Georgia Strait down through Juan de Fuca, often wandering into Puget Sound, or up the southwest coast of Vancouver Island, and along the western side of Washington as far south as Grays Harbour. From his home and lab overlooking Haro Strait, between San Juan and southern Vancouver Island, Balcomb uses spotting equipment and a hydrophone to intercept whales travelling to the Fraser River, the world's largest salmon-producing system. Like the northern researchers, he photographs orcas from a small boat.

It was quickly learned that the easiest whales to identify were the salmon-seeking residents, because of their predictable summer movements. It was also determined that resident pods mingle with one another, forming large groups, or "superpods," that travel, socialize, and rest together. Whales from the southern and northern communities, however, have clearly defined home ranges. They seem to respect an undrawn boundary in northern Georgia Strait: each community stays on its own side.

Resident pods may have from 5 to 50 members. At last count the northern community was comprised of about 190 whales from sixteen pods. The southern community has only three pods—J, K, and L—but they're generally larger than the northern pods, with a total of at least 90 whales. About half the southern orcas are members of L pod, the largest known pod on the coast.

All resident orcas are genetically similar and it's likely that pods interbreed, perhaps when they gather in superpods. Because of age and sex distribution, some pods couldn't possibly be self-perpetuating, but it is not known which males sire which calves. Although orca births have been witnessed in the wild occasionally, there is no proof of a human ever seeing killer whales mate. While some people claim to have seen whales having sexual intercourse, further investigation invariably shows what they had seen was actually homosexual activity among males. There's no question, however, that resident orcas exist in a matriarchal society, dominated by adult females.

Long-time observers of resident orcas see the same small groups within a pod always travelling together. A "maternal group"—a mother and her offspring—is the smallest component of a pod. Members of a maternal group are seldom more than a couple of hundred metres apart and are usually seen surfacing beside each other. They don't include adult daughters with offspring, which are considered separate maternal groups, but they may include post-productive grandmothers and adult sons.

"Subpods," comprised of maternal groups, are closely related—mothers, daughters, brothers, sisters, cousins. They are the "constant" in orca society, remaining together for their entire lives. In more than two decades of observation, an orca has never been known to permanently defect from one subpod to another. Because of this stability, researchers can document births and deaths in a population by examining the subpods.

Pods, consisting of a number of subpods, are whales that travel together almost all of the time, although maternal groups within a pod could be as far as seven or eight kilometres apart. Subpods may separate from pods for extended periods—a few days, weeks, even months; with observations limited to a short summer season, it's difficult to ascertain how long these separations may last. If a subpod contains animals of reproductive age, it could split along matrilineal lines to form a new pod, a process which probably takes several decades. With subpods separating from pods, then rejoining, then separating again, the question of when a subpod becomes a new pod continues to vex scientists— another reason for long-term monitoring.

Besides the residents there are another hundred-odd whales—the "transients"—which cruise in small groups from Washington to Alaska. Skin biopsies of captive and dead whales prove that residents and transients are genetically different races; it is believed they haven't interbred for a hundred thousand years or more. Movements of transient whales are

unpredictable, and sightings, compared to residents, are infrequent. They differ significantly in many respects: vocalizations, diving patterns, travel routes. There are even subtle differences in appearance: the tip of a resident's dorsal fin is usually rounded, with the front edge straight or curved back; a transient's dorsal fin is often pointed, with a slight bulge on the leading edge.

Early conjecture that transients were pariahs from resident pods has been discounted, but the make-up of transient family groups remains a mystery. Researchers shy away from the word "pod" when referring to transients: while they may be seen repeatedly swimming with the same whales, they also seem to switch companions more readily than residents. "We know nothing about transient whales compared to what we understand about residents," says Graeme Ellis.

But it is known that transients are the formidable foes of marine mammals—seals, sea lions, porpoises, and larger whales. They're also known to gobble the odd seabird. These are the "killer" whales that hold such notoriety in the writings of Charles Scammon and other mariners of the past. Although transients and residents inhabit the same seas, they show no interest in or enmity toward one another.

In the 1990 film, *Island of Whales*, Mike Bigg ponders this harmonious arrangement. "First, they don't mix. We've travelled with both races many times. Sometimes they'll get within a hundred yards of one another but the two groups really don't integrate. Secondly, they don't eat the same food, so they don't compete. Transients eat marine mammals and residents eat fish. So it's as though the two races have agreed on some sort of treaty—'I'll eat one kind of food, you eat another.' This way they can stay in the same area and not compete."

* * *

One of the most invaluable tools for killer-whale research is the hydrophone. It was used to locate enemy submarines during World War Two and much of the technology was developed in Pacific Northwest waters. Ships or aircraft would "deploy the pickle" and listen for the rumbling of moving submarines. Subs attempting to evade detection would lie quietly, motors cut, until the coast was clear.

It was old navy equipment that John Ford, a young graduate student, hauled up to Johnstone Strait in 1978 to begin his master's research on the vocalizations of orcas. Ford had done some recording of whales at the Vancouver Aquarium and analyzed the tapes with help from the Canadian Forces. In 1975 he was invited by Aquarium Director Murray Newman to the Arctic, where he moored a hydrophone offshore and recorded the underwater chatter of about three hundred narwhals gathered in a bay. The recordings were "an incredible array of jumbled sounds," and there was no way to tell which whale was making which sound. But he gathered enough data to earn an honours degree from the University of B.C. with a thesis on narwhal acoustics in the high Arctic.

He was more interested in killer whales than narwhals, however, so he paid a visit to Mike Bigg at Vancouver Island's Pacific Biological Station in Nanaimo. Ford suggested that individual pods could have specific dialects and perhaps the sounds were used by whales to tell one family from another. "I proposed that totally out of naivety because I didn't have a strong enough background in mammalian communication to realize that mammals don't have things like dialects at a group level. It just doesn't happen. I think

A "SUPERPOD" GATHERS IN ALASKA'S PRINCE WILLIAM SOUND. WHALES FROM SEVERAL PODS OCCASIONALLY MEET TO REST AND SOCIALIZE. SOME SCIENTISTS SURMISE THESE MEETINGS MAY BE ORCA ORGIES, A TIME WHEN PODS INTERBREED. AT THIS GATHERING MORE THAN SEVENTY WHALES FROM A NUMBER OF PODS APPEARED.

Mike understood that, so he thought perhaps I was a little bit off the wall."

Discouraged by Bigg's reaction, Ford let the killer-whale acoustics idea simmer for a while. During that time he got sidetracked by a gray-whale researcher from Tofino, on the west coast of Vancouver Island, who suggested to Ford that he study the feeding habits of gray whales. Apparently nobody else wanted to.

"I went out in May of '77 with Jim Darling to have a close look at gray whales and start thinking about how a project like that might work. The weather was disgusting; the gray whales were boring. So, disheartened, we came back into Tofino. We were tying up Jim's boat at the crab dock and two killer whales surfaced right beside the boat. Yikes! We jumped back in the boat and headed out after them. They went around the west coast of Vargas Island, two typical transients going right through the surf breaking on the rocks. I thought, 'Well, this is really what I want to do. These animals are so fascinating, so dramatic.'"

He and Bigg had discussed killer-whale acoustics a number of times since his original proposition and Bigg was warming up to the idea. Ford convinced UBC zoology professor Dean Fisher, who had supervised Bigg's doctorate research, to oversee a master's project. Bigg wangled some funding and a well-worn five-metre runabout, the *Brown Bomber*, and Ford and his wife loaded up and headed for killer-whale territory.

In those days there was no highway to the north end of Vancouver Island, and it was a sixty-kilometre run from Kelsey Bay up Johnstone Strait to Ford's base camp on Parson Island. Almost immediately, the old fifty-horse Mercury outboard broke down. After hasty repairs it functioned at about half-capacity. When Ford eased off the throttle, the boat nose-dived into the waves because the fuel tank was mounted in the bow. They commandeered a primitive camp established a few years earlier by Graeme Ellis, who'd been buzzing about in an inflatable Zodiac, looking for whales.

"The camp wasn't much," Ford recalls grimly, "just some tarps and my old family tent. We set that up inside an abandoned house that was there. It was a miserable summer weatherwise. We really discovered that Johnstone Strait can be a nasty place. Of course, you learn: we're better at it now." They were battered by an inordinate number of southeasters that year; with a none-too-trusty outboard, the grocery store at Alert Bay, twenty kilometres west of their camp, might as well have been on the far side of the moon. "We were getting down to jigging for bottomfish and subsistence foraging at low tide."

The photo-identification of whales was an integral part of his work: with the whales identified he would be able to match specific sounds with specific groups of animals, an advantage he lacked with his narwhal study. At that time, however, several northern pods were still unnamed, so Ford's project included helping amass the ID shots that were taking over Mike Bigg's office.

At the outset he found himself overwhelmed by his own enthusiasm. "I had a lot of ambitious theoretical questions, like trying to understand the use of sonar in whales." The boat was loaded to the gunnels with recording gear, underwater light meters, instruments for measuring turbidity. "I think all that lasted the first day. I just gave up on it. By the time I'd get ahead of the whales and set up the equipment, they were long gone." He realized his first chore was to get a handle on the logistics of his study, so he narrowed his focus to recording and photo-identifying the whales.

Another thing Ford learned early was that it's unwise to get involved in a tug-of-war with a killer whale. He dropped a hydrophone, attached to a thick cable, into about ten metres of water and wrapped the cable around a cleat. The boat suddenly listed to one side as a feisty whale yanked the hydrophone. The whale let go but followed the hydrophone up, rapidly clicking its sonar sounds into the tape recorder.

"I was hanging over the side of the boat, pulling up the end, expecting a couple of bare wires, but the whole hydrophone was still there. She came up with it, broke the surface and blew right in my face as I was hanging over the side looking at this hydrophone. It was enough to make me want to study mountain beavers."

During his first six-week field season, certain types of sounds were becoming familiar, but it was too early to interpret their meanings. Ford did, however, begin to think he was not as "off the wall" as Bigg had initially thought, that these animals could indeed have pod-specific dialects. The sounds he heard on days when the A pods were around differed from those he heard when B pod was in the vicinity, although the two groups share some calls. But a certain pod of "mystery whales" that Bigg had been unable to identify produced sounds quite different from A or B pods.

One day, in the autumn after he returned from Johnstone Strait, the entire southern community of whales showed up off the mouth of the Fraser River, following a big run of sockeye. Ford raced out in the *Brown Bomber* and managed to get them on tape. It was instantly clear to him that they sounded like a different species from the northern pods he'd been monitoring. "These animals sounded radically different."

When he returned to Johnstone Strait the next summer, B pod showed up within a few days. "I put down the hydrophone and started recording. Again, right away, I heard those calls I was now familiar with that were correlated with B pod's presence in '78. There they were again."

That's when Ford decided to record all the pods to see if each did, in fact, have its own dialect. He realized he'd never get the work done in the time he was given to complete a master's thesis, so he returned to his committee at UBC and persuaded them to support his Ph.D. research, a project that took until 1984.

Through his hydrophones Ford listened to whales for "hundreds and hundreds" of hours. He taped their clicks, canarylike whistles, and loud, complex calls that can be heard as far as fifteen kilometres away. Experiments on captive orcas show that they produce a series of rapid clicks for echolocation. Orcas have a special body of fat within the melon, a fleshy bulge in front of the head which has acoustic properties that focus high-frequency sounds into a cone-shaped beam ahead of the whale. Though an orca's ear canal is closed, it nonetheless hears with considerable sensitivity. When the echoes bounce back, the sounds penetrate the hollow bone of the mandible, then are conducted to the middle ear. The sound presents the animal with an image of its surroundings. The clicks, on which orcas seem to rely more than eyesight, are probably used to locate prey and to navigate tortuous channels.

The loud whistles and calls, produced through the nasal passage beneath the blowhole, seem to be a form of social signalling. Typically less than two seconds long, these squeals and screams are bursts of pulses generated at up to several thousand a second. By varying the timing of the pulses, orcas emit a variety of signals. Most pods have about a dozen "discrete calls," says Ford, which can be identified by ear. It appears orcas use their calls to stay in touch when out of sight of one another. They also exchange calls for several minutes when choosing a route at a junction of channels.

Calls vary with the situation, but no single call is always heard in a particular context. There isn't any consistent syntax to the calls either, but orcas seem to be prompted by one another: if one whale calls, another may respond with the same sound. Their vocalizations are more intense, higher pitched, with more rapid repetition, when two or more pods meet after an extended separation, activity that is frequently heard in Blackfish Sound through ORCALAB's hydrophones. Whales are especially loquacious when they congregate in superpods, infrequent occasions when as many as half the whales in a community meet. The specific calls of each pod are probably used at these meetings to keep individual orcas in touch with other members of their pod.

"There may be a real need for an elaborate set of sounds that are used as kind of a family badge, if you like, to keep the groups in contact," Ford explains. "They're travelling in large groups; they need to coordinate their behaviours, keep the group together, especially when they're mixed with up to a hundred animals."

These mass meetings may also be orca orgies, though the mating of wild killer whales has never been documented. It's possible that some pods may inbreed, but researchers believe it's more likely that pods crossbreed. Their calls may help whales determine whether they're related to one another. "So the dialect might be a mechanism by which they avoid inbreeding. By having twelve calls—that's an average for each resident group—they might encode lots of information about their relatedness. Perhaps only two or three calls wouldn't suffice to encode the amount of information they need to convey on identity and lineage."

Recording all this underwater dialogue seems almost easy compared to making sense of it. With extreme patience, a discerning ear, and a few gallons of midnight oil, Ford sat down to the tedious task of distinguishing one call from another. He began his analysis by ear, using his own system of hieroglyphics, strokes and squiggles representing the pitch contours of each sound. With a "real dinosaur" of an analyzer he then produced spectrograms of the sounds and wallpapered his office with them. Today he simply plays the tape into a sophisticated machine—a real-time spectrum analyzer—and produces an image, which he can freeze instantly, on a colour monitor. The calls have become so familiar that he can listen to any west-coast resident orca and name the pod.

"With the spectrograms, visually you could tell that the calls were different. I did the initial classification of the repertoires of calls of the groups based on visual comparisons. I could see that if certain pods shared calls that they had different accents on the calls. Some would make one part longer, or the other group would make it shorter. One pod might put an additional component on the end, a little ending part that other pods wouldn't make. I had to quantify that so I spent a full year measuring spectrograms."

Ford believes young orcas learn calls by mimicking their mothers. With females living as long as seventy or eighty years, there may be four generations in a single pod. As calls are transmitted across generations, variations appear. Some calls may change because of physical anomalies. "The whale might have a lisp, or something like that, and that becomes part of the way that animal makes the sounds. That carries on through subsequent generations."

ORCAS MINGLE IN THE SURFACE WATERS OF QUEEN CHARLOTTE STRAIT. THE WHALE IN THE CENTRE, JUST BELOW THE SURFACE, HAS ITS PENIS EXPOSED. THIS DISPLAY COULD BE HOMOSEXUAL ACTIVITY, WHICH IS COMMON AMONG YOUNG MALE WHALES.

Different pods that share some calls, with subtle variations, are members of the same "clan," according to Ford. A1, A4, A5, and B pods, for example, have similar dialects and are part of the A clan. I11 pod—Mike Bigg's "mystery whales"— produce entirely different calls from the A clan. R and W pods share some calls, so they are considered members of the R clan. The pods in a clan probably came from a common ancestral group that has split along matrilineal lines into separate pods over the centuries. Pods that share no calls likely have quite different origins.

The photo-identification of orcas can demonstrate how individuals within a pod are related, but it can't define the relationship, if any, of one pod to another. It would seem reasonable to assume that pods that spend much time together may have descended from the same ancestors, but that doesn't appear always to be the case.

"The acoustics tell a radically different story," says Ford. "Probably the dialects tell the true story of the ancestral history of the population." Certain pods with similar dialects, such as the three A pods, spend time with one another, yet others, such as C and D pods, seldom travel together although their dialects are "very, very similar."

"There are many examples of that throughout the population. The basic G pod, over the years of '73 through '83, were seen more often with B pod than with other groups in their own clan. Basically what the dialect relationships tell us is probably what the actual phylogeny of the groups might be, based on maternal descent."

Old recordings of west-coast orcas, collected before any whales were identified, support the assumption that orca calls may be passed through many generations before there's a noticeable change. J pod in the southern community, recorded by the Canadian Navy in 1958, makes the same sounds today. Shortly after Namu was caught in 1965, he rattled off the entire repertoire of C pod, his family in the northern community. Corky, a whale captured for Marineland in Los Angeles in 1969, still speaks the "language" of A5 pod. It wasn't until the early 1980s that these old recordings were matched to specific pods.

In one case, acoustic analysis led to the identification of another "mystery pod." Dean Fisher of UBC had recorded orcas in Johnstone Strait in 1964. Ford was into his fourth field season and had still not heard the "bizarre calls" of the whales on Fisher's tape. He speculated they could be a group tentatively called R pod, known from only one encounter in 1975. The sun was setting over Queen Charlotte Strait when Graeme Ellis ran across a mob of whales which hadn't been identified. Though conditions were poor, his photographs were sufficient to show these whales were unknown. They weren't seen again for six years.

Then, in 1981, Ellis and Ford were barbecuing dinner on Parson Island when they spotted whale spouts across Johnstone Strait, on the Vancouver Island side. They set off immediately in two boats, each intercepting different members of the pod. "I put down the hydrophone and made some tapes and there were those calls," Ford says excitedly. "Then Graeme called on the radio and said, 'This is R group.' It was like another revelation. Finally this is the missing piece of the jigsaw puzzle, the repertoire of sounds that was present in the mid-sixties. Here they were again. Of course, since then we have come to know Rs quite well...but that was only the second encounter with that pod."

Orca dialects are another phenomenon that emphasizes the profound differences between resident and transient killer whales. Researchers have identified fewer than half a dozen sounds shared by transient orcas distributed along four or five thousand kilometres of coast from California to Alaska. California transients have never been seen in B.C. or Alaska, or vice versa, yet their jargon is the same.

No one knows why transients manage with far fewer sounds. It is known that their groups are smaller and possibly not related in the same way as resident pods. Prey also could play a role. Residents, which vocalize profusely when hunting, feed on fish, which are probably not sensitive to the whales' underwater sounds. Transients are quiet when stalking seals, sea lions, or porpoises.

Ford's work was far from over when he was awarded his Ph.D. in 1984. Four years later, at the age of thirty-three, he was appointed Curator of Marine Mammals at the Vancouver Public Aquarium. Now the aquarium's marine-mammal scientist, he has since been analyzing orca recordings from Alaska. His ambition is to decipher the population structure of killer whales on the entire west coast of North America through acoustic analysis.

* * *

Just how many orcas inhabit the west coast of North America, or the rest of the world's oceans, is anybody's guess. They roam all oceans of the world, preferring temperate and colder climes. Although the most intensive killer-whale research has been carried out off the Pacific Northwest coast, orca studies have been done in Australia, Argentina, Iceland, Norway, and the Crozet and Prince Edward islands. Some populations have sustained sizeable harvests: Norwegians took 987 from their waters between 1954 and 1977, and the Japanese took 1,178 from their seas during the same period. The last major hunt was in 1979 and '80 when Soviet whalers took 906 orcas from Antarctic waters. The Soviet harvest prompted the International Whaling Commission to recommend a ban on orca whaling until more was known about the impact on the species.

It wasn't until the early 1990s that researchers in the Pacific Northwest began to look beyond near-shore waters. Perhaps there are thousands out there, whales that live their whole lives offshore. It's not uncommon for trans-Pacific sailors to see killer whales in the middle of the ocean. We know that only a few orcas patrolling B.C. waters swim to Alaska, and that none travel to California, but we have no idea where they go between sightings.

Southern-community whales are seen about twice a month in winter, says Ken Balcomb. According to his calculations, orcas cruising at an average of 3.5 knots could make a return trip of about a thousand kilometres between sightings. Balcomb has watched killer whales in Haro Strait devouring juvenile coho salmon heading out to sea. Growing coho spend significant time feeding in the plankton-rich waters over the continental shelf: it's a good bet that orcas are lured by salmon out to the edge of the shelf.

The outer edge of the continental shelf runs along the two-hundred- or three-hundred-metre contour. Off northern Washington and southern Vancouver Island that's about ninety kilometres from shore. Near the northwest tip of the island the shelf edge is about twenty kilometres offshore. Beyond the island it continues along the seaward side of Queen Charlotte Sound to the southern end of the Queen Charlotte Islands. On the western fringe of the Charlottes the shelf is virtually nonexistent, with depths plunging to more than twenty-five hundred metres a short distance from shore.

In the inside waters of Washington and B.C., twenty or thirty metres is a comfortable foraging depth for resident killer whales, although they're capable of feeding at depths of two hundred metres or more. One carcass was found off Vancouver Island, entangled in an underwater cable a kilometre beneath the surface, but it's unclear how it got there. On the continental shelf there are several particularly fishy banks—Swiftsure, Finger, Gullies, La Perouse, 6 Mile, Amphitrite, and others— which rise to within forty or fifty metres of the surface. Salmon, herring, groundfish, and other species thrive at these banks. In the waters around La Perouse Bank, thirty kilometres off southern Vancouver Island, annual catches of hake in the early 1990s were three hundred thousand tonnes, while groundfish catches amounted to more than a hundred thousand tonnes.

In 1990, while trawlers from Canada, the United States, Russia, Poland, and Japan were harvesting hake off La Perouse, a pod of about forty killer whales appeared. Photographs confirmed the whales were unknown to researchers. It's uncertain what they were eating, but their arrival coincided with the peak of the fishing season. Balcomb says he occasionally receives reports of whales at offshore banks: they could be oceanic whales that follow prey in from the open sea, or residents that move out from shore.

The resident orcas of Johnstone and Georgia straits have never been seen in the Queen Charlotte Islands, where in 1990 a large unidentified pod was seen by crew members aboard the sailboat *Island Roamer*. The next summer John Ford and his colleagues recorded two pods in the Charlottes, one of which spoke the dialect of the *Island Roamer* whales. The calls of the three pods differed from all the whales that Ford has heard farther south in B.C. or in Alaska. There must be at least another sixty "resident-type, fish-eating" whales. "They may be an offshore population that occasionally rubs up against the Charlottes," Ford speculates.

* * *

North of the Queen Charlotte Islands, research on Alaskan killer whales has followed much the same pattern as in B.C and Washington. Like their neighbours to the south, Alaskans showed little concern for their killer whales until someone expressed an interest in harvesting them. Short research stints were funded in the early 1980s when Sea World

announced plans to capture live orcas from Alaskan waters. More research was funded in the mid-eighties when fish-stealing killer whales began pushing black-cod fishermen to the verge of bankruptcy. Then, after the catastrophic oil spill in 1989, money for killer-whale research seemed to flow as thickly as crude from the ruptured hull of the *Exxon Valdez*.

In the early 1970s, Craig Matkin stored his surfboard and the beaches of southern California in his past and set off to find a future in America's most northerly hinterland. He had acquired a bachelor's degree at the University of California in Santa Cruz. The day after graduating, at the age of twenty, he hitchhiked up the coast and stopped at the end of the road—Homer, Alaska, where today Matkin and his young family are carving a homestead from twenty hectares of wilderness.

While surveying salmon rivers for the state of Alaska, he began to take an interest in killer whales he saw while travelling from stream to stream. In 1976, after reading in the book *Mind in the Waters* of Paul Spong kayaking amid wild orcas, Matkin found himself floating alone in a kayak with wild killer whales. In the restricted waters of Eshamy Lagoon, he watched with trepidation as two orcas and a false killer whale came "charging straight down the middle of the lagoon," right past him.

"I thought, 'Oh God, there's going to be a blood bath. They're chasing the false killer whale down and they're going to kill it.'" Preoccupied with the three whales, he hardly noticed as a female and several juveniles surrounded his kayak. "It really startled me. . . . I was definitely a bit nervous."

The whales at the end of the lagoon began breaching, then suddenly turned and crashed through the water toward Matkin and the other whales. Matkin feared they would rip the false killer whale apart right in front of him. But they didn't: they just congregated around his boat and rested until long after nightfall.

"It was great. I was there long enough to get the feeling of being with the animals," he recalls. "That was it. After that I decided I was going back to college at Fairbanks to study killer whales."

Matkin's research, however, was beset by a string of misfortunes. His cabin in the woods near Fairbanks burned down, so he slept on the floor of his lab, down the hall from a room where diseased animals were housed for study. Funding for killer-whale research was lurking on the horizon because Sea World was planning to capture Alaskan whales in 1977. But when Sea World decided to acquire Icelandic whales, the funding didn't materialize.

Matkin shelved orca research and decided to look into problems fishermen were having with seals and sea lions on the Copper River delta in Prince William Sound. He was hired aboard a fish-buying boat headed for the Copper River and later was taken

A YOUNG KILLER WHALE CATCHES A RIDE IN THE WAKE OF A FISH PACKER. ORCAS, THE LARGEST MEMBERS OF THE DOLPHIN FAMILY, ENJOY RIDING BOAT WAKES, PARTICULARLY OFF THE STERNS OF FREIGHTERS, CRUISE SHIPS, AND OTHER LARGE VESSELS. WHEN CREWMEN NOTICED THIS WHALE THEY TOSSED IT A FEW SALMON.

on as a deck hand on a seiner. He deduced that fishing could be as challenging a career as research and opted to do both.

He continued to fish and photograph killer whales while working on his thesis. He was awarded a master's degree for his seal and sea-lion work in 1980, a year that was a turning point in Matkin's life. While attending the first killer-whale symposium, in Seattle, he ran across Mike Bigg and John Ford. He showed them his most recent identification pictures and though they responded politely, Matkin could read the disappointment on their faces. They took him to Bigg's office at Nanaimo for a crash course on photo-identification.

Matkin bought a gill-netter that year and planned to continue snapping ID shots of killer whales while fishing. The boat also became a supply ship for Olga von Ziegesar, an undergraduate student of Ken Norris, studying humpback whales from a camp at Whale Bay, in southwest Prince William Sound. Von Ziegesar, who'd lived nearly half her life in Homer, was no stranger to Alaskan waters. Matkin looked forward to their periodic meetings when he'd run food and equipment to her camp. She became particularly attractive in 1983 when she received "a good chunk of funding" from the Alaska government for humpback and killer-whale work in western Prince William Sound.

Matkin leased his gill-netter to von Ziegesar and Beth Goodwin, both able mariners, who began the first systematic identification of orcas in the sound. Matkin leased a seiner and continued fishing and taking ID shots when he ran across whales. Some pods were becoming familiar, but it was clear an entire field season was needed to complete the identifications, which meant Matkin would have to forget fishing for a year. Graeme Ellis, whom they'd met earlier, agreed to help.

At the same time, Sea World came up with a new plan to take Alaskan killer whales for breeding and display in their four aquariums. They were given a permit to capture ninety whales and do biopsies, stomach lavages, tooth extractions, and some radio-tagging, then release all but ten. The permit could not be exercised, however, until more was known about the biology and population dynamics of Alaskan orcas. Matkin, von Ziegesar, and Ellis were the obvious choices.

"It was a bit of a moral dilemma because we were basically not in favour of live captures," Matkin recalls. "Graeme was certainly opposed to animals in captivity. I was a little more ambivalent, but I wasn't in favour of live captures. So it was a difficult situation." On the other hand, this was the financial break they needed to go full tilt into the collection of baseline data they'd been piecing together bit by bit. So they signed an agreement saying they would neither support nor oppose the project: they were simply scientists providing a service, hired to report on the numbers and social structure of killer whales.

A YOUNG CALF, HUNTING WITH A COW AND LARGE BULL KNOWN AS CHARLIE CHIN, APPEARS JUBILANT AFTER DEVOURING A SEAL IN KNIGHT INLET. SHORTLY AFTER THRASHING ITS TAIL ON THE SURFACE, THIS WHALE TURNED ITS ATTENTION TO A RHINOCEROS AUKLET, WHICH IT FAILED TO CATCH.

With the help of field assistants Kirsten Englund and Beth Goodwin, photographs were taken and shipped to Ellis every week or two in 1984. With sightings every other day, they shot ten thousand frames from April to September. Ellis, who by then had been photo-identifying whales for more than a decade, arrived in September, a time when superpods gather in the sound. As new photos were matched with others from previous years, the make-up of orca society in Prince William Sound began to emerge.

It appeared there were ten resident pods with a total of about 180 whales. Another group of about twenty-four have habits similar to transient whales in B.C., but they may feed on fish as well as marine mammals. Other whales have since been discovered and it's estimated today that more than two hundred whales travel in Prince William Sound.

While surveys were being conducted in Prince William Sound, Ken Balcomb and others were working in southeast Alaska. Today there are probably a total of sixty resident and seventy transient whales in that area. One pod from southeast Alaska occasionally swims into Prince William Sound. In addition to all these whales, another hundred or more inhabit the area around Kodiak Island, southwest of Prince William Sound.

With such a successful field season behind them, Matkin and his friends were stricken by the same "scientist's syndrome" that swept Mike Bigg into the world of whale research. They had become intimately familiar with numerous individual animals. "From then on it was unstoppable," Matkin smiles. "You can't let go. Once we did '84 it was all over, our fate was sealed: we knew we had to keep following these damn things."

Sea World was taken by surprise when the research they'd purchased became the basis for objections to live captures. When fishermen, environmentalists, and other Alaskans learned there weren't thousands of whales out there, that they were seeing the same few orcas over and over, they rallied to the rescue of "their whales." People familiar with the situation in B.C. and Washington during the mid-seventies saw a case of history repeating itself.

"In the frontier spirit of Alaska, where hunting is a major occupation and life is wild, Sea World figured they wouldn't have any problem coming up and taking whales," says Matkin, "but Alaskans basically said, 'What right have you got to take these whales? These are our whales.'"

Matkin and his colleagues were asked to publicly support the aquarium's position, but they refused, citing a clause in their agreement. Sea World funded further studies the next year, but the contract was awarded to a different researcher. The capture permit was challenged in court and rescinded.

Back to square one with research funding, Von Ziegesar and Matkin, who exchanged nuptial vows that year, formed a non-profit organization called the North Gulf Oceanic

Society. They raised money through donations; they sold pictures, calendars, and other whale paraphernalia, subscribing to the Balcomb School of Fund Raising.

"It was the same old Kenny Balcomb story," Matkin laughs. "That's what he started out doing. He used to sell anything that wasn't tied down. He was great: he'd go to these conferences and set up a little booth right in the lobby, selling all this stuff."

When killer-whale research funds are scarce, fishing is a mainstay for Matkin. While monitoring his boat radio during the 1985 season, Matkin heard fishermen complaining of killer whales robbing sablefish from longlines. These lines, some as long as two kilometres, are laid along the seafloor and anchored at each end. Buoys floating on the surface mark the anchors. Every metre or so a baited hook is affixed to the line to catch three- or four-kilogram sablefish, or Alaskan blackcod, as they are commonly known. The lines are often set in the morning and retrieved in the evening.

Blackcod are rich and oily, like sockeye—perhaps a delicacy to killer whales. They are deep-water fish which probably aren't part of an orca's usual diet. Certain whales in Prince William Sound learned to find easy meals by waiting near a buoy marking the end of a longline. "These whales would just sit in one spot," Matkin says. "You never see that; even when killer whales are resting they're always moving a little bit, going somewhere. These guys would just sit there and wait."

As soon as the winches began to turn, the whales were up to the boat in a flash, stealing the sablefish a boat-length off the side. It wasn't long before Matkin's ID shots were showing whales with bullet wounds.

The National Marine Fisheries Service in Juneau asked Matkin to talk with fishermen and determine which whales were the thieves. He interviewed twenty-two fishermen who reported a total loss in 1985 of 53,910 kilograms of fish, about a quarter of the potential catch. Another $26,285 worth of gear was damaged or lost.

When he went out to watch the killer whales' methods, Matkin was astonished. He pulled alongside a longliner and asked the skipper if whales were giving him trouble. The fisherman told him to wait ten minutes, and promised trouble.

"So he starts pulling his gear and says, 'Watch the horizon.'" Some two kilometres away a wall of foaming water was racing toward the boat: the researchers soon realized that thirty-five killer whales—all of AB pod—were bearing down on the boat, shoulder to shoulder, at seventeen knots.

The whales, leery of gunshots, stayed a safe distance from the boat, snatching fish below the surface. The longline came aboard picked clean, the odd fish jaw clinging to a hook, some hooks straightened out.

Most people agree the whales are alerted by sound, but no one is sure exactly what

sound. Tests were tried, using longlines with unbaited hooks, but when the dinner bell rang the whales ignored the lines. It's possible they actually hear the fish, or can tell when there's a load on the winches. Soon after the problem arose, John Ford and researcher Dave Bain began testing the hearing of captive whales at the Vancouver Aquarium to see if they could help find a solution.

Various techniques were tried to repel the whales. They found that orcas wouldn't take fish from either side of a tangle in a line. So "tangle imitators" were hung on the lines—and ignored by the whales. Seal bombs, used by fishermen to discourage seals and sea lions from swiping fish, were tossed toward the whales with no response. Acoustical harassment devices designed to frighten seals from fish hatcheries dissuaded the whales—once. "Then they figured it out. You got the feeling that these whales were just up for what's next."

They found the culprits were one group in particular—AB pod. Matkin would follow the whales until they were twelve or fourteen kilometres from the fish boat, then call the skipper and say it was safe to pull the line. As soon as the winches turned the whales would head straight for the boat.

AB pod is the "friendliest" in Prince William Sound, accounting for about 70 percent of the sightings. Matkin is more familiar with these whales than any others and it's obvious he views them with some affection. Matkin also has an uncommon ability to take his work seriously, but not get upset about things over which he has no control. While he's sympathetic to the longliners' predicament, he's noticeably amused by the orcas' mischief.

"You know they're playing games and everything you do is just egging them on because they like it. . . . This is where the true killer-whale personality really comes out. They're up for a challenge."

It was thought that if two fishermen several kilometres apart worked together, they could keep the whales dashing back and forth. The fisherman farthest from the whales would pull his gear and, as the whales zeroed in, he'd drop it back down. The other fisherman would then pull his gear, and the whales would turn around and head for his boat. This way the fishermen could haul in their lines in sections without the frustrated whales getting near the catch.

"It worked really well for a while," Matkin chuckles. "Then the whales split into two groups. It didn't even take them an hour to figure it out. They were so thrilled when they figured out what was going on, that we were playing games. They were breaching by the boats."

The consequences of all this high-seas sport, however, were not so humorous. At least eight whales from AB pod definitely bore fresh gunshot injuries in 1985 and another five appeared to be wounded. Six AB whales died in 1985 and '86. Three of the whales that died in 1986 were known to be carrying gunshot wounds the previous year. Mortality was four or five times the normal rate.

Although the longliners' dilemma remains unresolved, the shootings seem to have ended in 1987 after word drifted around the sound that the blackcod fishery could be shut down if the bullet-riddled corpses of killer whales didn't stop sinking out of sight.

Research was slow for a couple of years—until March 24, 1989. Matkin's thirteen-metre purse seiner *Lucky Star* was hauled up on the beach at Seward, a couple of hours' drive from his house at Homer. He was cramped up in the hold, installing a new fathometer, when a voice on the radio said an oil tanker had run aground in Prince William Sound. One of the world's worst ecological disasters was unfolding.

To Matkin, it was "just like they'd bombed Pearl Harbour." His livelihood, the place he had spent the past fifteen years, was threatened. In a panic, he collected two other fishermen and ran off to the closest U.S. Coast Guard station. All they knew was what they'd heard on the radio news: the *Exxon Valdez* had been impaled on a reef for nine hours; thirty million litres of oil were spreading across the sound and more was gushing through the punctured hull. "It was total chaos. All we got were conflicting stories. There was little or no activity going on out there. Nobody had any idea what to do."

A friend with a floatplane flew out for a look while Matkin worked frenetically, getting his boat ready to relaunch. His dismayed friend returned, visibly upset by the scene he'd witnessed—seals, sea lions, seabirds slipping through the oil-tainted ocean, unaware of the lingering death that awaited them. By the time Matkin had gathered his family and put his boat in, storm-force winds and high seas were predicted to sweep across the sound. The crippled ship had been spewing oil in calm seas for three days before the wind blew seventy knots, seas swelled to six metres, and Matkin sat helpless on shore.

"When it came down enough to go, the oil was everywhere. They'd missed their chance to do anything with it. It was gone." The sky was a muddle of helicopters and floatplanes; fish boats and patrol vessels steamed out of every port. Anyone with a boat was put on Exxon's payroll, at about $4,000 a day, whether or not the skipper wanted to work for the oil company. It was too late to seriously consider retrieving the oil, so they tried instead to protect the most ecologically sensitive areas. Fish hatcheries were a priority and Matkin headed for Port San Juan to help lay booms around a hatchery.

Wildlife authorities had heard a report that a group of transient orcas was swimming in the oil near the tanker. They needed help tracking down those whales and others in

RESEARCHER-FISHERMAN CRAIG MATKIN HAS WATCHED THE POPULATIONS OF KILLER WHALES IN PRINCE WILLIAM SOUND FLUC-TUATE. HE HAS WITNESSED THE EFFECTS OF SHOOTINGS BY ALASKAN BLACKCOD FISHERMEN, AND THE HAVOC WREAKED BY THE *EXXON VALDEZ* OIL SPILL IN 1989. (BRUCE OBEE PHOTO)

CAMERAS CLICK FURIOUSLY AS

ORCAS PASS A NUMBER OF

WHALE-WATCHING BOATS IN

WEYNTON PASSAGE, NEAR JOHN-

STONE STRAIT. WHALE-WATCHING

HAS BECOME A MAJOR INDUS-

TRY HERE, WHERE SOME TEN

THOUSAND PEOPLE TAKE TO

BOATS EACH SUMMER TO

SEARCH FOR WILD KILLER

WHALES. NO ONE IS SURE IF

THE ANIMALS ARE AFFECTED BY

THE HUMAN ACTIVITY.

the sound. Five days after the spill, killer whales were sighted off the south end of Knight Island as oil was oozing down both sides of the island. It was AB pod and Matkin photographed them through the day before he realized some of the whales were missing.

"We had a plane up above that was working with us, watching them. They said the whales were coming up right through the oil, not avoiding it at all. It wasn't thick crude, but they were moving through heavy sheens of oil. That's the way we left them that night."

When the photographs were analyzed by Graeme Ellis, he was upset because Matkin had failed to shoot every whale. Matkin couldn't convince him that he'd photographed all the whales that were there. Pictures taken later in the year confirmed that seven were missing. Then the entire pod disappeared for a couple of months, an unusual occurrence for AB pod.

AB pod had recovered from the losses in the longliner conflict and was up to thirty-six animals before the oil spill. Shortly after the spill, seven were gone. The next year another six vanished. Killer whales usually sink when they die, so there's no absolute proof that the whales are dead, and there's rarely a chance for a necropsy to determine the cause of death. But because of the social structure of resident orcas, it's fair to assume that whales missing for a couple of years are dead. As in British Columbia, no whales missing for at least two years have ever been seen again.

Matkin knew that AB pod was there, in the oil, right after the spill. It appears some transients suffered as well. "It gets to be a little stickier because their social system isn't so tidy. When transients are missing you can't just say that they're dead, but there's a great number of transient whales that we just aren't seeing any more, ones we used to see regularly before the spill."

With the exception of laying booms at the hatchery, Matkin didn't work for Exxon. During the height of the oil-spill confusion he told the company to take him off their payroll, something apparently no one else had done. Despite his instructions, he later received a letter saying that Exxon couldn't send his cheque until he provided a ship's log that briefly recounted his activities during the previous two and a half months. Then a friend called and said Matkin's cheque was sitting on a desk in front of him.

"Before it's sent out I'm supposed to get the okay from so and so," his friend explained, "but, you know, I could put this in an envelope right now and send it to you. Nobody'd ever know, or care. What do you want me to do?"

"Ah, Jesus," Matkin replied. "I can't do that. No way." The cheque was for $280,000. Now, when Matkin scrounges around for research money, the memory of that cheque gnaws at his integrity. "You fool!" is Graeme Ellis's repeated admonition, and nobody's really sure if he's kidding.

It will probably be years, even decades, before the effects of the catastrophe on the whales and wildlife of Prince William Sound are known. It didn't take long, however, for Alaskans to see what a precious and temperamental natural gift they have, one that could be so profoundly affected by their industrial endeavours.

"We hadn't realistically assessed what would happen here, as fishermen, any more than the oil companies had. We just counted on the fact that someone else was taking care of it," says Matkin. "We just thought it was a one-in-a-million chance and it wasn't going to happen.

"We felt pretty foolish when it did. Here we are, the state of Alaska, getting huge sums of money because of this pipeline. You think there aren't going to be any repercussions, but you don't get away with things like that in the end. We all began to realize that this oil money isn't free money."

* * *

In 1976, the year Matkin decided to study killer whales, Ken Balcomb came onto the scene in Washington. Like Matkin, Balcomb had earned a zoology degree at the University of California. He then began graduate work in anatomy, concentrating on the respiration of marine mammals. In 1963, while working at the university's veterinary school during the day, he was a government biological technician at night. Sizing, sexing, and documenting stomach contents of whales landed at a station near San Francisco, he had a first-hand look at the interior designs of humpbacks, blues, fin whales, grays, sperm whales, orcas, and other species taken by whalers.

After a decade as a navy pilot and antisubmarine warfare specialist, Balcomb returned to whale work, carrying out the first American field study of Washington's killer whales in 1976. The next year he sailed out of Boston Harbour as an employee of the Ocean Research and Education Society, studying whales in the North Atlantic. He returned to Washington each summer to count killer whales and report his findings to Mike Bigg and his other Canadian colleagues. In 1985 he established a permanent home for the Centre for Whale Research on San Juan Island. Like Bigg, Matkin, and the others, Balcomb has kept up his orca work with volunteer help and minimal funding.

"Funding? We've never had significant funding." He received $31,000 in 1976 to launch the program and another $7,000 in 1978, the last year he was given government support. "Governments respond to emergencies," says Balcomb. "They're in a firefighting sort of mode—something fires up, they go and dump money all over it and hope it dies down. They haven't perceived an emergency in something that is as stable, and apparently growing right now, as the southern population of killer whales."

But there are fisheries questions involving killer whales to which both the American and Canadian governments have turned a blind eye. "They actually remain remarkably silent about that whole fisheries interaction issue." There's little that fishermen can do about killer whales that compete for salmon, short of eliminating the whales. In 1992 the U.S. National Marine Fisheries Service was asking Congress to authorize the killing of whales by fishermen to protect their catch. In Canada it is illegal to kill a wild whale for any reason.

When Balcomb presented the situation from the whales' perspective, suggesting that fisheries managers should allot a portion of the catch to orcas, they thought he was joking. "I don't think it's been seriously thought about by any of the management regimes that we have in place today. They have no mandate for it and it's probably never occurred to them." But Balcomb estimates that orcas in the southern community alone could devour forty-five hundred to nine thousand kilograms of salmon a day—possibly as much as three million kilos a year.

It's up to fisheries managers, says Balcomb, to ensure killer whales have sufficient prey to survive, yet as we watch fish stocks decline along the coast of North America, only the consequences for fishermen are considered. The American Fisheries Society says that 214 natural spawning stocks are "at risk" in Washington, Oregon, Idaho, and California. All stocks have declined since the turn of the century and 30 percent of salmon stocks in the entire eastern North Pacific are dropping drastically today.

As salmon stocks decrease, orcas turn to other, less desirable prey. When A9, a fifty-eight-year-old northern resident, died in 1990, her stomach was full of bottomfish. "As these whales have to eat more non-salmon types of fish, particularly bottomfish, they're going to be exposed to all the sorts of things that those bottomfish are carrying—mercury, cadmium, other heavy metals, PCBs, DDTs. All the stuff that's in the benthic community is going to be bioaccumulated in the predator. The whales may be able to deal with toxins in terms of individual survival, but cumulatively it will adversely affect their reproductive success."

Orcas may continue to find food a thousand kilometres offshore, says Balcomb, but if we wipe out the salmon stocks, whales and other predators will become a rare sight along the near-shore waters of the Pacific Northwest. "The fact is, as I see it, these whales will not be here in the middle of the next century if we continue to live our lifestyles as we do right now."

* * *

Meanwhile, back at Telegraph Cove, Jim Borrowman is baking his bones on the roof. "Here," he grunts, "feel how heavy this bugger is." The jawbone of a killer-whale skull is hooked around his bathroom vent to prevent the bone from slipping down the roof. Borrowman slides it up over the vent, almost falling backwards into his eaves troughs. "You can see where I've numbered all the teeth." He points at pencilled numbers beside each gaping hole of a toothless mandible and explains that the teeth are in his pantry, soaking in a jar of olive oil. "Keeps them from cracking."

Skulls, flukes, vertebrae, and an assortment of other bones are scattered across the roof, bleaching in the summer sun. "The pectoral fins are over there," he says, pointing to the shingles on his woodshed. "Now that we're up here you could help me turn them over." He squats at the bottom of a long line of bones and methodically works his way up the roof, carefully turning each bone as he climbs.

This killer whale was a gift from Mike Bigg. "Mike called and said, 'I've got just the right size for you—it's a medium.' A whale that weighs six or eight tonnes, well, how do you deal with it? This one weighed just barely a tonne: it was perfect." Bigg wanted to do a necropsy to find out why it died, but first they had to get it. It had been found floating near Namu, a 180-kilometre run from Telegraph Cove. Borrowman and his partners in Stubbs Island Whale Watching had just taken delivery of their new eighteen-metre whale-watching boat, the *Lukwa*, so they took the seats off the aft deck and headed up the coast. "The boat was brand-new, hadn't even done a whale-watching trip. So the first spectator on the whale-watching boat was a whale."

They did the necropsy on a beach around a point from Telegraph Cove, then wrapped the carcass in chicken wire and sunk it in twelve metres of water to let the crabs and crustaceans pick at it for a year. Now, after the bones have dried for a year on the roof, Borrowman scratches his head, trying to figure out how to assemble the skeleton: it didn't come with instructions.

"That's the Steller's sea lion," he says, nodding toward a garbage can on top of his oil tank. "I had to put him up there because of the bear." Lately a black bear has taken to wandering the boardwalk along the edge of the cove, just before midnight when the sport fishermen are comfortably ensconced in their Winnebagos in the campground up the hill. The bear sniffed around the trash can, then flattened it to pop off the lid. "But when he found what he had he wasn't too interested."

The sea lion was a "floater" that Borrowman dragged ashore and tidied up before adding it to his bone collection. "It was enough to gag a maggot; he was pretty stinky. I rubbed a little perfume in my nose before I started on him, but that doesn't really help. . .I cut him into three bite-sized pieces so I could handle him. He wasn't all that big, about eight or nine hundred pounds. Once I flensed him all down to the vertebrae and head I could carry him back here in three or four chunks with most of the meat off.

"I put him on the office roof. What I tried to get going on him was a nice brood of maggots because they'll eat it all up, clean it up really good. But it didn't take; the maggots didn't get going on it and the meat hardened and dried. That's going to be a lot of work getting the meat off the bones."

"C'mon over to the office," he says, climbing down the ladder. "I'll show you the gray whale." At the end of the boardwalk, past the clapboard houses and flower boxes, the boat sheds and gift shops, I follow Borrowman onto an aluminum roof over the Telegraph Cove post office. "I've got the whole thing," he beams, studying his bones admiringly. This whale, much larger than the killer whale, was a gift from John Ford and his wife, Bev. They found it washed up on a beach in Goletas Channel, near Port Hardy. Most of the flesh had rotted and they loaded as many bones as they could into their boat and delivered them to Borrowman. The rest were stashed in the bush above the tideline and taken a year later to join the other defunct marine mammals at Telegraph Cove.

Borrowman plans to complement their whale-watching business with a museum of all the marine mammals indigenous to local waters. He keeps a few extra bones handy to barter with other collectors. At the moment he has his heart set on a Dall's porpoise and a false killer whale. If anyone's got one, he'd be happy to swap it for a sea lion. . .or a Pacific white-sided dolphin. . .perhaps an orca skull. . . .

A decidedly odd avocation. How did he get into it?

"Just a fluke."

A YOUNG FEMALE ORCA BREACHES IN JOHNSTONE STRAIT. BREACHING WHALES OFTEN PROVIDE AN OPPORTUNITY FOR RESEARCHERS TO SEX ANIMALS BY PHOTOGRAPHING GENITAL SLITS. NO ONE KNOWS WHY WHALES BREACH, BUT SOME OBSERVERS BELIEVE THAT WHALES OF THE PACIFIC NORTHWEST'S SOUTHERN COMMUNITY BREACH MORE OFTEN THAN THOSE IN THE NORTH.

* * *

"Let's get rollin,'" Graeme Ellis shouts from the dock below the Telegraph Cove post office. His small cruiser is tied alongside the *Lukwa:* the motor's running and Ellis is anxious to cast off. At the top of the dock Borrowman's partner, Bill Mackay, is doing his spiel for a group of whale-watchers about to board the *Lukwa.* Mackay's wife, Donna, has her ear glued to the phone in the office, while Anne Borrowman is putting the finishing touches on lunch for forty. Jim Borrowman is politicking along the boardwalk, acting like the mayor of Telegraph Cove, population twenty-two. As usual, he's sporting his blue shorts, the ones he puts on in May and wears until the first frosts of October.

Ellis is in the cockpit of the boat, fiddling with a camera lens. A curly-haired kid in his forties, he's eager to get on the water and find his whales. He's in his element behind the wheel of a boat, tracking the animals he's known for half his life.

We're headed for Echo Bay, on the northwest end of Gilford Island, where Alexandra Morton lives with her young son, Jarret. I've been looking forward to meeting this woman. I'd read of her in newspapers and magazines, seen her in documentary films, and had heard of her talent for spellbinding audiences with her illustrated talks on killer whales. The "whale lady," they call her, probably a fitting honorific.

It's the end of the field season and Ellis has photographed most of the animals he'd expected to find. He'd like to shoot a few miscellaneous whales, preferably away from the whale-watchers, fishermen, and pleasure boaters in the hub of Johnstone Strait. We head around the western end of Hanson Island through Weynton Passage into Queen Charlotte Strait. Off Lizard Point, on the backside of Malcolm Island, we deploy the pickle but hear only the *kthump, kthump* of a fish boat chugging past Broughton Island, ten kilometres away.

"*Lukwa*, G.E.," the radio crackles. We recognize Bill Mackay's voice.

"Yeah, Bill," Ellis replies, "what's up?"

"Guy off the end of Gilford says he saw black triangles. Looked like two or three."

"Did he say which way they were headed?"

"No," Mackay replies, "but we're going up to Retreat Passage for a look. There's nothing else doing. We've been down to the bight and it's dead."

"Okay," says Ellis. "Lemme know."

Ellis consults a chart and sees a labyrinth of reefs and islands between our position and the whales. He checks his watch, then scans the sea with his binoculars a full 360 degrees. I've learned to stop pestering him with my persistent questions when he's figuring the whereabouts of whales.

"Blackfish Sound, Graeme," the radio calls.

"Hello, Alex," Ellis says into the microphone.

"We've got three transients up at Cramer Pass."

"Which way are they going?"

"Looks like they'll either go through Arrow Passage or down into Retreat."

"Thanks, Alex. Seen any others?"

"Not today. I've been canning all day. These ones came by the house so I went out after them. Are you guys coming for dinner?"

"Affirmative," Ellis replies, "soon as we finish up out here."

We weave a course through the warren of waterways off the southwest end of Bonwick Island and head into Retreat Passage on the island's eastern side. Across the pass on Gilford Island the Indian reserve at Health Bay is a cluster of weatherworn shanties and beached fish boats. Farther up, Alex Morton waves from the cockpit of her boat and points in opposite directions. The whales have spread out and are working the shorelines along both sides of the pass, slowly swimming our way. Eventually the three come together and Ellis readies his camera.

"*Lukwa*, G.E.," Mackay calls. The *Lukwa*, with a full load of whale-watchers, is drifting off Health Bay, waiting to intercept the whales.

"Looks like Charlie Chin's group," says Mackay.

"Yeah," replies Ellis, "haven't seen old Charlie here for a while." Like other transients, this group is nomadic. For the past three years they've been seen near Glacier Bay, Alaska, in June and off southeast Vancouver Island in September.

Ellis hoists his three-hundred-millimetre lens into position and presses the camera brace against his shoulder. By the time he can get a good shot we've moved between the whales and the *Lukwa*. With four dozen people glaring down from the decks of an eighteen-metre cruiser, Ellis feels self-conscious about approaching the whales and getting on with his work. I'm reminded of a comment by Mike Bigg in the film *Island of Whales*.

"It's an interesting change in attitudes. When we began in 1973 people were shooting at them. It was a fairly common thing. But we went out just a few days ago and I felt I had to apologize to the whale-watching boat, that I was in photographing these whales to identify who's born and died out of a particular pod, and that I wasn't harassing them. So it's gone from worrying about harassing from shooting, to worrying about harassing through research."

But Mackay explains Ellis's purpose to his passengers and tells them of the killer-whale study that began here in the early 1970s. Many wave as they head back toward Johnstone Strait to look for other orcas. Ellis and I stay with the three transients, a big bull—Charlie Chin—a cow and a young calf. Their pace quickens as they swim around the southwest end of Gilford Island into the mouth of Knight Inlet.

Penetrating 113 kilometres into the western slopes of the Coast Mountains, Knight

BORROWMAN'S BONES. THE ROOFTOPS OF TELEGRAPH COVE ARE EMBELLISHED BY AN ASSORTMENT OF MARINE-MAMMAL BONES COLLECTED BY JIM BORROWMAN, OF STUBBS ISLAND WHALE WATCHING. BORROWMAN'S HOPE IS TO CREATE A MUSEUM OF MARINE MAMMALS INDIGENOUS TO THE AREA. (BRUCE OBEE PHOTO)

Inlet is the second-longest fjord in British Columbia. Mount Waddington, at 4,016 metres the province's highest peak, rises above the head of the inlet. The glaciated waters of the Klinaklini, Franklin, and Sim rivers feed the upper reaches of the inlet and another seventy streams tumble down from the forests as it snakes toward Queen Charlotte Strait. The precipitous hillsides that flank the inlet's shores plunge far below the water's surface, reaching a depth of 549 metres.

The three whales mosey along the southern shore, poking around nooks and islets as they move farther up the fiord. Ellis makes several attempts to position the boat for an ID shot of Charlie Chin's left side, but the uncooperative orca keeps diving under the boat and coming up on the other side.

"C'mon, Charlie, you big ugly fish," Ellis hollers, trying to keep pace with the whale.

"Do you think that whale knows you were the one who caught him and penned him up at Pedder Bay?" I ask.

"Hope not," Ellis shudders.

Suddenly Charlie Chin turns full circle and darts into a cove on the starboard side of the boat. The cow and calf are splashing in a frenzy of foam as Charlie dives, then resurfaces tail first. There's more splashing before we see the telltale cloud of blood staining the waters of the cove. The cow, her dorsal fin just below the surface, swims alongside the boat, a big chunk of fresh red flesh in her mouth.

"Get that with the dip net," Ellis yells, pointing to something that's quickly sinking from view. I reach down and scoop the intestines of some unfortunate seal or porpoise.

"What is that?" Ellis inquires.

"Looks like someone's stomach," I reply. "Did you see anything?"

Except for a few seabirds we'd seen nothing that resembled a killer whale's lunch. Yet somehow they had detected their prey and devoured it before our very eyes, all within the space of two minutes. It's common for orcas to batter seals or sea lions with their flukes, or ram them with their bodies for as long as a couple of hours before eating them. But we'd witnessed nothing so dramatic: it was all over in a flash.

The whales seem pleased with themselves after their meal, spy-hopping, breaching, tail-lobbing, as they continue their hunt up the inlet. Charlie Chin breaches a few metres off the port side. The others stop abruptly in front of the boat. Again there's a great deal of commotion, splashing, flukes slapping. The two whales move right against the rocky shore, then slip out of sight. We wait, ten seconds, fifteen, twenty-five seconds, then the mottled grey body of a harbour seal pops through the surface, its terrified eyes bulging from its head. The cow appears right behind the seal and comes down on its victim with open jaws. Like the first kill, it's over in minutes. Charlie moves in for his share as they rip the hapless seal to shreds.

"They must be teaching the little one how to hunt," Ellis suggests. "Seems to be doing all right."

Again the whales celebrate their success with a sensational display of breaches and tail slaps. "Look at that," cries Ellis. Off our stern an hysterical rhinoceros auklet is flapping over a kelp bed with the little calf in hot pursuit. The bird flutters past the boat while the whale races behind like a hydroplane. The auklet dives and the calf gives up the chase.

A brisk breeze is puffing up the inlet and the trees along the shore begin to sway. Choppy seas and whitecaps are a signal to seek a safe haven. We bid the whales farewell and head for Echo Bay, at the eastern end of Fife Sound.

Smoke spirals from the chimney of a float house where Cramer Pass opens into Echo Bay. On a rocky shore above the float house, Alex Morton waves from the porch of her cottage. Her house too was a float house until recently when she hauled it up the bank above the sea. "You can see where it split," she says, peering under the house at a large crack in a support beam. Inside, the canner is still steaming and venison burgers are cooking on the wood stove. Indian carvings hang from the ceiling, and the walls are embellished by silk-screened fish, paintings, whale photographs, and several of Morton's own drawings. Her son, Jarret, has a friend staying for a few days, another of the eleven children who attend the little school at Echo Bay.

Morton has been watching the whales of the northern community since 1979, helping provide identification photographs for Mike Bigg's ongoing study. Her particular interest is behavioural differences between residents and transients. Unlike most orca researchers, she lives permanently in the heart of killer-whale territory where she can study the whales year-round. A hydrophone anchored in front of her house transmits the calls of approaching orcas to a monitor in her kitchen. With camera, notebook, and portable hydrophone she follows the whales for as long as daylight permits.

Morton has never been paid for her work, and after years of studying the whales she still can't define her motives. "I just know that they intrigue me immensely and there's no other motivating force in my life. I've thought that maybe I should just be a photographer, a writer—concentrate on one of the other things that I'm doing. But boy, if I hear there are killer whales going by I'm just beside myself. I have to get out there."

Her obsession with killer whales is an idiosyncracy shared by many, if not most orca researchers. The extent of the obsession varies, but it seems to stem from something beyond simple research, a kind of mammalian bond between human and whale. These whales have families like ours, yet they symbolize an unfettered freedom that most people are unable to enjoy. Maybe it's envy, or emulation, but there's no question that to Alex Morton and others like her these orcas are more than just research animals: there's a deep-rooted concern for the welfare of the whales.

A native of Lakeville, Connecticut, Morton became interested in whales at the age of twelve after reading the works of John Lilly, a California doctor who published books on communicating with dolphins. Born into a family of artists, at eighteen Morton worked in the graphics department at ABC Television in Washington, D.C. The future in television, however, was Los Angeles, so she moved to the west coast, only to find the TV job prospects bleak. "The low point was when I was doing scoreboards for roller derbies in downtown L.A. It was pretty bad."

Her life took a new direction when she was "awestruck" at a lecture by John Lilly: she made up her mind to work for him. When her first letter received no reply, she drew Lilly a sketch combining the faces of a dolphin and a human looking through the same eye. Still no response. So she called and talked Lilly into inviting her to his home.

When she finally met him in person, Morton found John Lilly to be a "really imposing character," Morton recalls. Despite her nervousness she was hired to paint a mural in Lilly's house. At the end of the hallway where she worked was a closed room; inside, an air conditioner ran constantly. One day the door was left open: in the room were wall-to-wall audio tapes, layer after layer. Morton knew they had to be the tapes from his research. "That room just called to me."

When the mural was finished she spent weekends for the next two years cataloguing Lilly's tapes, listening to them as she worked. Intrigued by dolphin communications, Morton asked the curator at Marineland of the Pacific if she could do a dolphin study on the relationship between sounds and behaviour in dolphins. The park was closing for a few months and the curator was concerned the dolphins would get bored. He granted permission for Morton's study and asked if she'd swim with the dolphins to keep their spirits up.

While Morton was doing her study at Marineland, Corky, an orca taken from B.C. waters in 1969, gave birth. But the calf soon died and Corky fell into a deep depression. She would sink to the bottom and repeat the same vocalization endlessly. "It ignited the awareness in me that captivity had a certain wrongness about it, and that my race had violated this mother whale in the most basic sense."

For three days Corky ignored a call made repeatedly by the male orca. Finally Corky responded to the male's call and eventually began to eat and swim. "I saw that they actually had a relationship," says Morton.

She worked with the whales and dolphins for several months, holding jobs with the U.S. Navy and the San Diego Natural History Museum. She'd heard of John Ford's

work on whale dialects and was interested in Mike Bigg's study, so she called him. "Mike just blew me away. He was extremely cooperative, offered all the help he could. He even sent pictures of Corky's family."

Before long her worldly belongings were piled into a Zodiac at Alert Bay, where she waited for Paul Spong to escort her to ORCALAB. While someone was helping her start the outboard, a pod of orcas swam past the Alert Bay dock. She cast off and followed them, dropped the hydrophone and heard the calls she'd recorded so often at Marineland. It was A5 pod, the family from which Corky had been separated a decade earlier.

Later that year, while in a boat near Hanson Island, Alex was approached by a man who said he and a partner, Robin Morton, were shooting a film at Robson Bight, where killer whales come to scratch their bellies on the gravel bottom. They wanted a shot of a researcher watching the whales. Alex accepted the invitation and was dropped on the beach to wait for Robin, who was underwater.

"Robin just kind of walks out of the water—it was just incredible—I'm watching this guy as he peels off his dry suit. He's got this tattooed Indian killer whale on him. I'll tell you, he had my attention. . . . I just completely fell in love."

They were married in 1980 and soon had a son. Home was the *Blue Fjord*, a boat which they had purchased and chartered out while working on films along the coast. After a charter in the Queen Charlottes they spent the summer in Johnstone Strait. They had been looking for somewhere they could watch whales year-round, but most people were vague when asked if they saw whales in winter.

"We came up right into Fife Sound and there were these little float houses with smoke coming out of them. They looked so warm and cozy. We couldn't believe there were people living back here. To me, entering these inlets was like going off the edge of the planet. It looked like a wilderness. I was amazed that I could even find my way with the charts."

ALEX MORTON CHECKS HER OUTBOARD MOTOR, ESSENTIAL EQUIPMENT FOR LIFE IN ISOLATED ECHO BAY. MORTON, AUTHOR OF THE AWARDING-WINNING BOOK *SIWITI—A WHALE'S STORY*, HAS CONTINUED THE WORK SHE BEGAN WITH HER HUSBAND, ROBIN, WHO DIED IN 1986 WHILE PHOTOGRAPHING ORCAS UNDERWATER NEAR ROBSON BIGHT. (BRUCE OBEE PHOTO)

FORTY-FOUR INTERLOCKING, CONE-SHAPED TEETH ARE USED BY KILLER WHALES TO GRASP AND TEAR THEIR PREY, WHICH IS SWALLOWED IN LARGE CHUNKS. STORIES OF ORCAS WITH "RAZOR-SHARP" TEETH ARE EX-AGGERATED: AN ORCA TOOTH CAN BE COMPARED IN SIZE AND SHARPNESS TO A LARGE HUMAN THUMB.

Their son, Jarret, had spent little time with other kids. So in 1984, the Mortons set up in the tiny outback community of Echo Bay, where there's a post office, store, school, scheduled air service, and year-round access to Johnstone Strait. Charter work paid the bills, but the Mortons were always torn between film-making and research. Eventually they decided to sell the boat and buy a float house.

The Mortons had saved enough to continue their research while Robin went back into full-time film-making. On September 16, 1986, Robin was diving with whales near Robson Bight, using a rebreather system. Alex and Jarret were in the boat. There was an unwritten agreement that Robin would not be interrupted while filming underwater. When whales approached the bight he usually surfaced to ask Alex where they'd gone. On this day, A9, an orca they'd known a number of years, swam toward the bight, then suddenly turned around and dashed away, followed by other whales. Alex became suspicious when Robin didn't surface a few moments later to inquire about the whales. "When that time elapsed I was still hesitant...then he just didn't surface."

"The rebreather is a controversial piece of diving equipment that allowed him to swim underwater without emitting air bubbles," Alex later wrote in a magazine article. "He had used it many times before, but this time a tiny valve became clogged, reducing the flow of oxygen. As Robin breathed, the self-contained system continued to supply him with a normal amount of gas mixture, but the percentage of oxygen quickly dropped.

"Tragically, the human body gives no warning in this situation; when the level of oxygen in the blood drops too low, unconsciousness results immediately. A diver has no chance to reach the surface or signal for help—and he drowns. The whales gave me the only indication that something was wrong by their unusually quick departure. I dived in and brought Robin to the surface, but I was too late. He had died among the whales he loved, a hundred yards from where we had first met."

Bill and Donna Mackay took the young widow and her son in at Telegraph Cove and helped them through the next few days. Many people automatically assumed she would leave her remote home, but she and Jarret have comfortably settled into their isolated lifestyle. They're careful to avoid accidents—dangerous tools like the chainsaw stay in the shed if the weather's too poor for an emergency evacuation. And Morton's not so frightened of the bears that come down to the back door at night, now that someone has taught her how to fire the rifle. "But I'm not totally convinced there are no sasquatches," she grins.

Morton expects to move from Echo Bay for a few years when Jarret is old enough for high school. But they'll likely return, and until then the whales provide all the motivation she needs. "Everything about killer whales seems to have some purpose. There always seems to be intent behind what they do. There's mystique. I wonder about them, about how much they're perceiving about what goes on around them."

Simply learning about whales is enough satisfaction for some researchers, but Morton shares her knowledge with others in the hope of promoting a better appreciation of west-coast orcas and their environment. Her magazine articles, photographs, and a children's book, *Siwiti—A Whale's Story,* help people understand modern-day killer whales and the everyday perils they face. She takes her late husband's films and her photographs to community halls, schools, or theatres and entrances audiences with her stories of wild orcas.

"If people look at a group of whales and you tell them that this is a mother and her two daughters, this is a son, and a grandma, people understand because you're using terms that relate to them. They know how they feel about their grandmothers...so they can see that the whales have these bonds as well. It seems to be a point of contact for people with whales."

* * *

Another point of contact for people with whales is Robson Bight, where orcas congregate to rest, to socialize, and to scratch their itchy bodies on the pebble seafloor. The bight encompasses the estuary of the Tsitika River, which flows into Johnstone Strait nineteen kilometres east of Telegraph Cove. It is one of the few known areas in the world where orcas regularly rub on the bottom of the sea. In summer killer whales come here almost every day.

No one knows why they rub; perhaps they scrape parasites from their sensitive skin, or maybe it's just for a good scratch. Neither transients nor residents of the southern community use rubbing beaches. Some Alaskan whales are known to enjoy this pastime, but on the B.C. coast only resident whales of the northern community indulge in rubbing. Though a few other rubbing beaches exist, Robson Bight is the favourite for 90 percent of Johnstone Strait's resident whales. A half-hour rub is average, but some skid along the bottom for a couple of hours or more. Through a hydrophone it sounds like buckets of marbles rolling down a street.

Robson Bight was not protected from industrial development until the early 1980s, and even then its preservation was ensured only after bitter disputes between loggers and conservationists. Forest companies had been systematically working their way up Johnstone Strait toward the Tsitika, clearcutting the east coast of Vancouver Island, watershed by watershed. Today the logged patches between the few remaining trees look like mange on a dog. Although new growth is "greening up," much of this area remains a hideous eyesore in the midst of what is becoming a busy international tourist destination.

In the late 1970s MacMillan Bloedel, B.C.'s forestry giant, was planning to turn the Tsitika estuary into a booming ground and dry-land sort. "They wanted basically to industrialize the last pristine bay and estuary on the east coast of Vancouver Island," says Jim Borrowman. Few people were aware of Robson Bight's importance to killer whales or its significance on a global scale. The Tsitika Integrated Resource Plan, in fact, didn't even acknowledge the orcas' use of the bay.

Borrowman had moved from Victoria to the north island, where he was working as a carpenter in Port McNeill and taking underwater photographs of killer whales in his spare time. Bill Mackay, also from Victoria, was working in the Telegraph Cove sawmill and spending a lot of time fly-fishing the Tsitika River. Neither was particularly enamoured with the idea of Robson Bight and the Tsitika estuary becoming a log-sorting area, so they sought the advice of Dr. Bristol Foster, B.C.'s Coordinator of Ecological Reserves.

A LONE ORCA SURFACES BENEATH THE MISTY FORESTS OF ROBSON BIGHT, AT THE MOUTH OF THE TSITIKA RIVER. THOUGH THE WATERS AND SHORELINE OF THE BIGHT ARE PRESERVED, THERE HAS BEEN CONTROVERSY OVER THE EFFECTS OF UP-STREAM LOGGING.

Make Robson Bight a public issue, said Foster: force the government to respond. Borrowman, Mackay, John Ford, and others involved were reluctant: the whales' serenity would be disrupted; tranquil Telegraph Cove would be swarmed by tourists. But the logging companies and Social Credit government of the day were old friends: the unsightly swaths of burnt stumps that stretch the length of Vancouver Island are clearcut evidence of their environmental priorities.

So the campaign began in earnest. A poster was printed bearing the words "Why Save the Whales if You Destroy the Habitat." Newspapers, politicians, and MacMillan Bloedel were inundated with letters; Robin Morton's stunning footage of orcas rubbing underwater was shown to cabinet ministers. The biggest boost came on September 20, 1980, when a killer whale gave birth before a pack of news reporters on a tour of Robson Bight.

"If you're going to go public, it's pretty hard to beat that kind of attention," Borrowman grins. "It made front page in all the papers." Two years later the provincial government established Robson Bight Ecological Reserve—1,248 hectares of ocean. By 1989, 505 hectares of upland property, including the entire Tsitika estuary, had been added. The name was changed to Robson Bight (Michael Bigg) Ecological Reserve two months after Bigg's death. Though Robson Bight and the Tsitika estuary now are legally protected, loggers and conservationists continue to argue whether siltation and other hazards of upstream logging will deter whales from using the bight.

With the new reserve came regulations to guarantee peace for the whales. The small pockets of gravel beach along a ten-kilometre stretch of shoreline are out of bounds to boaters, picnickers, and campers. Whale-watchers are expected to keep their distance when whales are there. Permits are required by researchers or anyone with a reason to enter the reserve. Now, thanks to their own hard-won campaign, the walks that Borrowman, Mackay, and others once enjoyed on the Tsitika estuary are cancelled.

"But I'll never regret the establishment of the reserve. I think it was very important," Borrowman says. As predicted, the sleepy backwater settlement of Telegraph Cove has become a summer tourist mecca. Borrowman, Mackay, and their wives formed Stubbs Island Charters in 1980, taking whale-watchers and scuba divers aboard the seventeen-metre *Gikumi*, a wooden-hulled cargo carrier.

Since starting the business the Borrowmans and Mackays have supported the study of wild whales. They take students and researchers aboard their boats; they contribute countless photographs for the identification of killer whales, and report their observations to scientists monitoring orca pods in their area. They occasionally haul whale carcasses from beaches and help researchers carry out necropsies. Mackay and Borrowman spend more time among wild orcas than the biologists studying the whales.

In 1989, when business was up to about four thousand passengers a year, they invested nearly $1 million in the *Lukwa*, specifically designed to carry a busload of tourists. Cruise ships and charter boats now make Telegraph Cove a regular stop. Anglers, competing with whales for salmon, fill a 120-site campground from May to October. By the early 1990s, as many as three thousand kayakers were launching from the cove each summer. In 1991 the cove's historic sawmill was bulldozed to make way for more tourist accommodation.

Whether all this traffic bothers the whales is debatable. To explore the question, a federal-provincial Johnstone Strait Killer Whale Committee was struck in 1990 to assess

A YOUNG CALF SURFACES BE-TWEEN A LARGE BULL AND A MATURE FEMALE. THE SMALLEST COMPONENT OF AN ORCA POD IS A "MATERNAL GROUP," CON-SISTING OF A MOTHER AND HER OFFSPRING. THIS TRIO COULD BE A MOTHER WITH HER CALF AND AN OLDER SON.

the impact of people on whales and their environment and to recommend ways to ensure that Johnstone Strait remains prime orca habitat. Gone are the days when these same governments hoped machine guns and mortars would scare the whales away.

"I honestly don't see that the whales are concerned about all the hubbub," says Borrowman. "I wish they could read the newspapers. They'd probably be in tears with laughter over all this fuss."

Nonetheless, Borrowman sees the potential for harm if whale-watching remains unregulated. Commercial tour operators should be licensed, he says, and those who misbehave should have their licences pulled. Companies with large boats reduce traffic by taking large numbers of people to the whales in a single vessel. Experienced operators are also familiar with whale behaviour: they know when their presence becomes intrusive, when to back off and leave the whales alone.

Commercial whale-watching trips should be educational as well as entertaining, and operators have a responsibility to keep abreast of research developments. Borrowman and his partners have been members of the West Coast Whale Research Foundation since the early '80s. "I really think it's important that people know this stuff. You don't take them for five hours, just run out there and let them stand around watching these things come up to breathe, then take them back to the dock," he says.

The first report of the Johnstone Strait Killer Whale Committee says that in 1989 ten thousand people took tours aboard commercial whale-watching boats. These boats, however, are a minor part of the traffic. The Canadian Coast Guard says Johnstone Strait now is the busiest waterway on the B.C. coast. Most conspicuous are the fish boats: with as many as 140 fishing at once, they account for 85 percent of the vessels in Johnstone Strait during the commercial season. But fish boats are only part of the traffic. Throughout the year, tugs with barges and log booms, government vessels, freighters, oil tankers, cruise ships, pleasure boaters, anglers, paddlers, sailors, and ferries plug the waters of the strait.

From the kitchen table at ORCALAB I watch a steady stream of seine boats flowing in and out of Blackfish Sound. Through the hydrophone monitor, all those engines create a bothersome cacophony. The aggravating hum is punctuated by the grating "eeeerrr" of speedboats whizzing past the hydrophones. As Helena Symonds explains, it's not the physical presence of the growing marine traffic that is so worrisome, it's the unending invasion of the orcas' acoustical world.

"It's gotten to the point where the more hydrophones you put out the more boat noise you listen to and the uglier it gets," she says. "It makes you tense; you start being cranky. We know from listening that our own tolerance is going down all the time. We

have the option of turning it off: the whales don't. They're listening to that right now."
She gets up from the table and turns down the monitor.

Symonds and Spong often record orcas at night when boat noise is reduced. But by the crack of dawn speedboats are racing to the fishing spots, places often shared with foraging whales. "When I first came here, on a weekend day in the middle of summer there might have been one guy out there and I probably knew who he was. That was sports fishing," says Spong. "Now it's so crowded, incredibly crowded."

Spong wonders if there is an impact from all this noisy boating activity. Old-timers remember long lines of whales from several pods stretched across the surface to rest, a sight seen only occasionally now, he says.

"It's so difficult for them to get a rest any longer. There are always boats on them, always people pursuing them, always noise around them. I think it's a real change for them." Whether the change is harmful is something that can be determined only through long-term observation of the animals' behaviour.

TELEGRAPH COVE, ONCE A SLEEPY BACKWATER ON THE NORTHEAST COAST OF VANCOUVER ISLAND, HAS BECOME A SUMMER TOURIST MECCA SINCE THE ESTABLISHMENT OF ROBSON BIGHT (MICHAEL BIGG) ECOLOGICAL RESERVE IN 1982. NOW SEVERAL THOUSAND SPORT FISHERMEN, KAYAKERS, AND WHALE-WATCHERS HEAD FOR JOHNSTONE STRAIT FROM TELEGRAPH COVE EACH YEAR.

Spong advocates more land-based orca observation as a means of reducing traffic and noise. A trail could lead from Telegraph Cove to vantage points along the east coast of Vancouver Island, for example, with an interpretative centre, video relays, and hydrophones. Whale-watchers could be transported to the most reliable sighting spots on islands, where they'd spend the day on land rather than buzzing about in boats.

"The whales have very sensitive ears, especially at frequencies far higher than humans can hear," says John Ford, who shares the concern of Symonds and Spong. "What appears to our ears to be noisy is maybe not as irritating to them. But still it makes me wonder."

Increasing noise has compelled Ford to work away from areas like Johnstone or Haro straits. "You often can't even hear the whales with your hydrophones over the noise. . . .You go down to Haro Strait and it's even clearer how noisy we've made these waterways. Haro Strait usually has at least one freighter going through it and freighters are really noisy. That and all the small sports-fishing boats that have high-pitched prop noise. One wonders how these animals can function with that kind of noise regime."

Another recent addition to the underwater clamour are acoustic seal-scaring devices at fish farms. They scream like sirens into the water. Whether these gadgets are vexing to orcas wasn't considered when they were developed, says Ford.

* * *

No one knows how killer whales are affected by all this new noise and traffic, or by the many other changes we've brought to their habitat. Two decades, most researchers agree, is not long enough to determine what is "normal" behaviour for an orca: perhaps another twenty years are needed to prove whether the lives of today's whales really are hindered by human activities.

With the accumulation of knowledge, however, comes a greater diversity of opinion. Whales in captivity, the issue that enticed the scientific community to the wild orca's domain, seems no closer to resolution than when the studies began. In fact, our growing understanding of wild whales may have further divided opposing camps: while antagonists continue to call for freedom of the whales, supporters argue that without the education provided by captive orcas, the shoot-on-sight tactics of the past could reappear.

Most concede that captures of wild killer whales, certainly off the coast of North America, are history. So with that score settled, the gist of the controversy has progressed to a new realm. Now there's a call for the release of today's captive orcas: aquariums face mounting pressure to return their incarcerated whales to the oceans from which they were seized.

Paul Spong, since his 1969 dismissal from the Vancouver Aquarium, has been at the forefront of the freedom fight. In recent years he has pressured for the release of Corky,

now at Sea World in San Diego. According to Spong's plan, the whale would be held in a net pen in Blackfish Sound where she could become reacquainted with her original habitat and learn how to catch live fish again. When A5 pod swims by, Corky would be released and, it is hoped, accepted by her old family. Sea World, as expected, has flatly refused.

There is also disagreement among professionals. John Ford believes a captive whale would lose its place in the social system of the group, especially after an absence of twenty years. Once taken into captivity, it becomes a permanent member of the community of captive whales.

The captive whale issue won dubious prominence in February, 1991, when Hyak, a twenty-five-year-old orca at the Vancouver Aquarium, died. Then, four days later, a young trainer at Victoria's Sealand of the Pacific was killed by three captive orcas. Although unrelated, these incidents suddenly put animal-rights activists before the public eye.

They argued that Hyak's confinement was the cause of the whale's supposedly premature death, citing Mike Bigg's study which says bull orcas may live fifty or sixty years. The same study, however, says that 43 percent of wild orcas die within the first

(FOLLOWING PAGE) TWO RESIDENT ORCAS SURFACE NEAR A SAILBOAT IN JOHNSTONE STRAIT. ONLY TWO DECADES AGO MANY BOATERS WERE AFRAID OF KILLER WHALES AND OFTEN HEADED FOR THE SAFETY OF SHORE WHEN THEY APPROACHED. TODAY PEOPLE WHO SEE WILD WHALES CONSIDER THEMSELVES FORTUNATE.

year and males that survive live an average of twenty-nine years. Another argument was that unsanitary conditions cause fungus and bacterial infections, which often kill captive orcas. But there's no scientific backing for the claim. It is possible that wild whales die of similar ailments, but scientists rarely find a fresh enough carcass to determine the cause of death. It is known that the immunity of cetaceans is relatively weak compared to other animals: they have small lymphatic systems for animals of their size and could therefore be susceptible to infections or disease.

One obvious difference between captive and wild whales on which animal-rights advocates capitalize is the "flaccid-fin syndrome" in aquarium whales. It is particularly noticeable in males—their prominent dorsal fins are weakly flopped to one side, as if deflated, creating a sickly image. Scientists surmise that gravity and swimming patterns—around and around and around—contribute to this disorder, but there's no suggestion it's a sign of ill health. This odd aberration has been noticed only a few times among wild orcas, whose dorsal fins stand upright.

While there is no proof that confinement of orcas is physiologically harmful, it undoubtedly causes psychological stress, according to Spong, who was called as an expert witness at the inquest into the death of Sealand trainer Keltie Byrne. The twenty-year-old champion swimmer accidentally slipped into the orca pool; as she tried to climb out, she was pulled back by a killer whale. Before she drowned, three orcas tossed her about for ten minutes and one carried her underwater in its mouth. Spong testified that the whales' "bizarre and abnormal" behaviour was undoubtedly due to their confinement in "a condition of extreme sensory deprivation." On occasion one of these whales would be segregated from the others, often for medical reasons, in a small metal tank hardly bigger than the whale.

"You're not seeing a normal orca when you're looking at a whale in a tank," says Spong. Orcas rely largely on echolocation and a whale in a tank is cut off from its typical acoustic environment. "It's terribly, terribly monotonous." Trainers have been injured by whales in other aquariums, he says, adding there has never been a verified unprovoked attack on humans by wild orcas.

In spite of the opposition, some aquariums continue to search for sources of new whales, but it is becoming increasingly difficult. Iceland is rumoured to be considering a permanent ban on

live captures, so Russia is being eyed as a possible new supplier. And prices are up substantially from the days of Griffin and Goldsberry. A Canadian oceanarium would likely pay about $140,000 for an Icelandic orca if one was available. Prices are much higher for aquariums in the U.S., where American law imposes tight restrictions on the importation of killer whales. Sea World reportedly purchased a whale in 1990 from a British aquarium for close to $1 million.

But orcas must be a good investment. At the Vancouver Aquarium, with an array of fish and marine life, sea otters, beluga whales, seals, and tropical gardens, killer whales are by far the main draw. Hyak, captured in 1968, was seen by fifteen million people. In 1992 the Vancouver Aquarium announced it would no longer take wild orcas for public display, but would rely on North American breeding programs. In extraordinarily ambiguous wording, a report released with the announcement suggested the aquarium would support the capture of live whales if they were needed as "founding stock" for captive breeding.

"Our interests are the same as a museum; they are scientific and educational," Murray Newman says, adding that the aquarium spends almost $1 million a year on education and research. "We look at the Vancouver Aquarium as a reflection of nature. The significance of the aquarium is to make people think about ecology, to make children think about what exists in nature."

Children are most responsive to live whales, and once their curiosity is aroused

A THIN FILM OF WATER ENVE-LOPES A KILLER WHALE AS IT CHASES FISH NEAR THE SUR-FACE. THE WHALE, SWIMMING IN TIGHT CIRCLES, DIVED WITHOUT EXHALING, LEAVING SCATTERED FISH SCALES AS EVIDENCE OF ITS SUCCESS.

they are eager to learn more of the broader picture, of the ecological needs of whales and other marine life. Each year some fifty thousand school children come to the Vancouver Aquarium. As generations change, Newman says, there must be ongoing education to bolster a fundamental feeling that the animals displayed in captivity are worth saving in the wild. Books and films provide some insight, but nothing compares to a killer whale in the flesh. "To see them, hear them, smell them, there's a major difference and I think for young kids that is the hook," says John Ford. "Seeing the real thing, they develop an emotional bond. I'm not just spouting the company rhetoric here. My little nieces and nephews come in all the time and they're just hooked on these whales. I walk back and forth to my office many times a day and see the children who come here. Maybe the argument that we're teaching them the wrong message—it's okay to capture animals and hold them in these sorts of settings—has some merit to it. But I don't think so."

The aquarium is its own worst enemy, Ford continues. As youngsters, people fall in love with whales at the aquarium; as adults they want to release them. Then they say there's no need to continue keeping captive whales; there's nothing more to be learned. "That's fine for us to say because we grew up with whales around us in oceanaria. But if kids coming along today, the next generation, are not growing up with the animals, if they're not down here in their school groups seeing the living animal up close, I think they're going to lose that bond that can only be established by seeing the real thing."

Although Ford's career has been built mainly on field work, he recognizes the

THE TERM "FLACCID-FIN SYN-DROME," A DISORDER COMMON AMONG CAPTIVE WHALES, IS PERHAPS A MISNOMER. AL-THOUGH THIS DORSAL FIN AP-PEARS FLOPPED TO ONE SIDE, IT IS ACTUALLY RIGID IN THAT POSITION: IT'S UNLIKELY A HU-MAN COULD PULL IT UPRIGHT. SCIENTISTS SURMISE THAT GRAVITY AND CIRCULAR SWIM-MING PATTERNS CONTRIBUTE TO THIS DISORDER, BUT THERE'S NO SUGGESTION IT'S A SIGN OF ILL HEALTH. (BRUCE OBEE PHOTO)

opportunities that captive whales provide for research that can't be done with wild orcas. Even Paul Spong admits he has benefitted from his work with the aquarium's whales. "I think it's okay to have a few animals captive for the masses to see, provided the institution is credible and that a very strong effort is put into research, education, and conservation," says Ford. "My personal preference supports what the aquarium here is trying to accomplish: it's a non-profit society and part of the proceeds of having the animals here are put directly into research, not just here,

THE DORSAL FIN OF A MATURE
BULL ORCA IS ABOUT TWICE THE
HEIGHT OF A FEMALE'S FIN. FE-
MALES AND JUVENILE MALES
LOOK SIMILAR UNTIL THE MALE'S
DORSAL FIN BEGINS TO
"SPROUT."

but also in the field. That's one area of the aquarium's work that's rarely publicized."

Peter Hamilton, executive director of Lifeforce International, wholeheartedly disagrees. "You really have to question how valuable the Vancouver Aquarium is to the study of whales and other marine life. I think the purpose of the aquarium is to make money from the tourism and entertainment industry. . . . I think keeping captive whales desensitizes children to respecting these animals. It teaches them that it's okay for us to imprison whales just for our amusement."

A former commercial artist, Hamilton formed Lifeforce in 1980 to oppose the use of animals for "eating, experimenting, and entertaining." The organization promotes replacing the "marine-mammal slave trade" with rescue centres where sick or injured wild animals would be rehabilitated and released. With the backing of his two thousand members, Hamilton is the prickliest thorn in the side of the Vancouver Aquarium.

In 1990 Lifeforce unsuccessfully tried through the courts to block the aquarium's capture of three beluga whales. News reports indicated there was widespread public support for Hamilton's cause, but a survey commissioned by the federal government suggests otherwise. In 1989, before the capture permit was issued, pollster Angus Reid surveyed fifteen hundred Canadians on their opinions about aquariums and captive white whales. Seventy-one percent favoured the capture of live whales for viewing and education. The strongest support—80 percent—was from British Columbia. Seventy-five percent endorsed whale research in aquariums. Again B.C. offered the strongest support with 82 percent.

This survey, however, was about belugas, not killer whales, and public sentiment about catching wild orcas for display could be quite different. The pure white beluga, with its placid, grinning face and docile manner, is mesmeric; it has a hypnotic appeal. Killer whales, on the other hand, are the most suspenseful of all marine mammals, bursting through the surface with plumes of mist erupting from their blowholes. They have a

commanding, militaristic appearance as they plough along at speeds up to fifty kilometres an hour. They are the epitome of wild, free spirits.

There is no way, says Hamilton, that an aquarium can provide for the physical and social needs of such an animal. Survival of captive orcas has not been good, he says. While some have lived twelve, fifteen, even twenty years or more, others have died within five or six years. Some have lasted only months.

It is difficult to compare wild and captive mortality rates, says Ford, because there aren't enough captive whales to get a comparative sample. Certainly early mortality was significantly higher in the 1970s when aquariums were developing husbandry methods for their orcas. With today's knowledge, aquariums are better able to monitor the health of captive whales, to detect infections or illnesses at an early stage, to develop their own antibiotics. The calibre of aquariums varies: a study by U.S. researcher Dave Bain suggests that in the last decade mortality in aquariums with good track records is about the same as the mortality of wild whales.

In B.C. and Washington waters normal death and birth rates were thrown out of kilter by the captures in the 1960s and '70s. "There's definitely a skew in the age structure of the population as a result of those captures," says Ken Balcomb. "We know from the measurements of the animals removed and the ones that died that awfully young animals were taken, fifty-some whales, both sexes."

So a large group of whales that were young and saleable in the late 1960s and early

A HUMPBACK WHALE RAISES ITS PECTORAL FIN AS A TRANSIENT ORCA PASSES IN PRINCE WIL-LIAM SOUND. THE TRANSIENT, WHICH MAY DINE ON LARGER WHALES, APPEARED TO LOOK OVER THE HUMPBACK BEFORE BREACHING AND MOVING ON.

'70s are missing. "They would have been reproducing in the early '80s," Balcomb says, adding, "We not only lost them, we lost their potential offspring, the ones they would have added by now."

Balcomb estimates there were 112 orcas in the southern community before the captures. After his first census in 1976 there were 68. In 1991, when J pod produced two new calves, there was a total of 92 whales. If the captures hadn't occurred and the habitat's carrying capacity remained at 1960s levels, he says, there would probably have been 130 or 140 orcas in the southern community in 1991. "If the habitat can be maintained, I think we're going to reach a point in about another twenty or thirty years where we'll have basically a normal population again."

Balcomb, who founded San Juan Island's popular Whale Museum at Friday Harbour, has no qualms about voicing his views on captive whales. "We have to go with the flow of our own morals. I think in the sixties that the lion-tamer ideal of the killer whale in captivity was popular. The explosion of the myth that they were dangerous to man, the worst thing to fear in the sea, was a positive step in educating people. But I think we're evolving away from the concept of keeping wild animals in confinement for any reason. Is it now really a moral thing for us to take animals from their wild and free environment, snatch them away from their family and society, and put them in tiny artificial environments for either our education or entertainment? I think it is not."

On the issue of captive whales, Balcomb's and Ford's friend, Graeme Ellis, who, like Spong, admits he learned a great deal from his aquarium work, wonders if the "juice is worth the squeeze." In the early days, separating a whale from its pod was like catching a big fish or taking a kitten from a cat. Now, however, people know pods and individual whales by name; they know a whale's history and family relationships. "I don't think anyone could go out and take one of these animals. You can't do it now without taking someone you know. Can you go out and break up a family knowingly now, or remove an animal that you've watched so long in the wild? It'd be like removing an offspring from a human family."

It's obvious the public will no longer tolerate

the capture of live whales, so the solution for aquariums is breeding programs. During the formative years of whale husbandry, few captive-born calves survived. But since 1985, aquariums in both Canada and the U.S. have enjoyed a number of successful births.

Whales born in captivity are doomed to a life of imprisonment with no chance of parole, according to Paul Spong. "Many of these animals are genetic mixes; they have been born of Icelandic female and Pacific Northwest male parents." If Spong could ever convince aquariums to release their whales, those that are a mix of Icelandic and Northwest whales couldn't be set free without risking the contamination of existing genetically pure wild stocks. "If they went out of business, what would you do with the animals? One thing we don't want to do is risk the wild populations."

Jim Borrowman, whose livelihood depends largely on wild orcas, seems an unlikely defender of captive whales. But children, he says, easily become bored watching the dorsal fins of wild whales from a distance. They prefer aquariums, where they can view whales at close range. He is convinced that if aquariums stop educating children, the growing appreciation for wild orcas will diminish: the unenlightened attitudes of the 1960s could return. "It would be nice if there were no captive whales, but I'm afraid of what might happen in the future without them."

Alex Rhodes, owner of Sea Coast Expeditions in Victoria, agrees that watching wild whales is "adult-oriented," but disagrees that captive orcas inspire an appreciation of whales on the high seas. "We try to keep the experience in its proper context, to make sure people understand we're dealing with wild whales, not animals that are friendly towards humans."

Along with eight other passengers I join Rhodes in Victoria aboard his seven-metre high-speed inflatable boat for a trip across Haro Strait to San Juan Island, thirty kilometres away. As we're scouting along the southern shore, suddenly the dorsal fin of a big bull emerges from the sea, not ten metres from the boat. It's followed by a smaller whale, and biologist Pam Stacey, our orca interpreter, recognizes the stubby fin and unusually loud breathing. This is Spieden, officially J8, a grandmother estimated to be nearly sixty years old. Stacey confirms the identification from a photograph in her genealogical catalogue. The bull, she says, is Spieden's brother, Ralph, known by some as J6. Three other whales from this family—Spieden's thirty-four-year-old daughter, Mamma, and her two offspring Blossum and Shachi—are swimming off our starboard bow.

There are others, and Stacey explains that we are surrounded by J pod, four matrilineal groups totalling eighteen whales. Cameras click furiously as the killer whales entertain us, spy-hopping, breaching, flapping flukes and pectoral fins on the surface.

"This is the best seventy dollars I ever spent," says a beaming Mark Greaves, who travelled from England intent on seeing wild killer whales. A member of Greenpeace

A "SPROUTING" MALE KILLER WHALE PLAYFULLY SOMERSAULTS IN THE STORM-TORN WATERS OF JOHNSTONE STRAIT. AS YOUNG BULL ORCAS APPROACH SEXUAL MATURITY IN THEIR LATE TEENS THEIR DORSAL FINS "SPROUT" TO THEIR FULL SIZE, AS HIGH AS TWO METERS. THIS WHALE IS PROBABLY ABOUT FIFTEEN YEARS OLD.

U.K., he considers the confinement of whales cruel, and steadfastly refuses to view them in aquariums.

I envy his decisiveness, but I still find myself swaying between opinions on both sides of the issue. I've witnessed the excitement of my two young daughters as they peer through the glass at the Vancouver Aquarium into the tiny eyes of live orcas. I've shared their apprehension and awe at the sight of wild killer whales approaching our boat as we cruise the waters of southern Vancouver Island. Yet while my pragmatic side appreciates the value of captive whales, my emotions say it's wrong. These are not fish: they are families, like ours. We have the ability, but do we have the right to separate them? Today, with wild whales blowing a stone's throw from the boat, I feel my pragmatism yielding to my emotions.

Elated, we reluctantly head back to Victoria. As we pass Gonzales Bay, my childhood turf, I recall shooting at those dangerous beasts with our slingshots—we were lousy shots—and it seems my desire to fire at them has somehow faded with my adolescence and ignorance. It wasn't until today, listening to Pam Stacey, that I realized in forty years as a native islander I've watched this pod of whales many, many times. My own children have seen the offspring of the same wild whales I knew as a youngster. Two families, growing together on the same coast.

A SOLITARY ORCA SPY-HOPS IN THE SUNSET OFF MALCOLM IS-LAND. AN ORCA'S EYE, SLIGHTLY LARGER THAN A HUMAN EYE, IS COATED IN A PROTECTIVE MU-COUS. KILLER WHALES SEE WELL BOTH ABOVE AND BELOW THE SURFACE.

Pacific Gray Whales

Trails of silt cloud the waters of Finnerty Cove, where a Pacific gray whale is foraging three or four metres below the boat. I'm impatient, watching bubbles break above the whale as it ploughs along the bottom, straining tonnes of tiny invertebrates through its bony baleen plates. Suddenly a barnacle-encrusted snout bursts through the surface and a pungent plume gushes from its blowholes. We wince as the fishy fetor of recently swallowed whale food drifts downwind and sprays our faces.

"See what it's eating," says biologist Pam Stacey. She reaches into the water and scoops a handful of wiggling shrimplike things which the whale has churned up from the bottom. "Amphipods."

Prodigious as it may seem, this whale is only about three years old. In five or six years it will weigh about thirty tonnes and measure twelve or thirteen metres long. Even now it is well over twice the length of the boat: it could capsize us with a quick flip of its flukes.

The whale, however, appears undisturbed by our presence. It swims fluidly, making four or five shallow dives, blowing between each. Then it raises its enormous tail almost

THE ENORMOUS FLUKES OF A GRAY WHALE CATCH BOATERS BY SURPRISE AS THEY RISE ALMOST WITHIN TOUCHING DISTANCE. SCIENTISTS WONDER IF INCREASING MARINE TRAFFIC ADVERSELY AFFECTS MIGRATING AND FEEDING GRAY WHALES. SO FAR THE WHALES SEEM UNPERTURBED BY THE GROWING NUMBER OF HUMANS ON THE SEA. (JOHN FORD PHOTO) out of the water and rolls headlong into the depths, exposing the row of bumps, or knuckles, at the base of its back.

A woman on shore signals to us and asks if there's room for her in our boat. This is the fourth day she has perched on the rocks to quietly watch the great leviathan blowing and diving, blowing and diving, swimming in slow motion, unconcerned with its silent audience.

This whale at Finnerty Cove, in Haro Strait, is a bit off course. It really should be travelling up the outer west coast of Vancouver Island. Between late February and early May about twenty-one thousand Pacific, or California, grays migrate past the island to summer feeding grounds in the North Pacific and Arctic oceans. About a dozen usually stray through Juan de Fuca Strait into Haro and Georgia straits. They hang around all summer, then join the southbound migration sometime between November and January. These inside-water whales are often young: they've been seen amid the busy traffic of Vancouver Harbour and Puget Sound, and poking around the lower reaches of the Fraser River. A few others stop to feed at the mouths of mainland inlets near the north end of Vancouver Island, while another forty or so spend the summer feeding off the island's west coast. The majority of North America's Pacific gray whales, however, migrate beyond Washington and British Columbia, through the Gulf of Alaska to the Bering and Chukchi seas, where they feast until autumn ice floes begin to force them south.

The incredible sixteen-thousand-kilometre return migration of the Pacific gray whale is one of the longest of any mammal on earth. It begins at breeding grounds in Mexico's Baja California. Travelling alone, in pairs and trios, or in groups of twelve or fifteen, the first migrants—newly pregnant cows—are moving past central California by mid-February. They're followed about two weeks later by mature males, anestrous females, and juveniles. Cows with calves are last to leave, usually in mid-March, though some stay in the lagoons as late as early May. Although they may travel in groups, Pacific gray whales, unlike killer whales, do not form close-knit pods which stay together for life. Once a calf is weaned at about nine months old, like a bear cub or seal pup it is left to fend for itself.

Often swimming within a kilometre of shore, these whales are prime prey for naturalists. From Mexico to Alaska, whale-watchers gather on rocky promontories and boat decks to scan the seas for telltale spouts. Gray whales, with their extensive range and such healthy numbers, are "watched" by more people—literally millions—than any other cetacean on North America's Pacific coast.

As remarkable as the gray whale's migration is its near-miraculous return from the brink of extinction. The historic population of fifteen or twenty thousand was hunted relentlessly by nineteenth-century whalers. By the mid-1870s they had all but vanished.

A SPY-HOPPING GRAY WHALE SURVEYS ITS SURROUNDINGS WITH ITS TINY EYE, LOCATED NEAR THE UPPER END OF ITS JAWS. UNLIKE KILLER WHALES, GRAY WHALES DO NOT USE ECHOLOCATION, SO IT'S PROBABLE THAT GRAYS RELY PARTIALLY ON SIGHTINGS OF THEIR TERRESTRIAL SURROUNDINGS TO NAVIGATE. (JIM BORROWMAN PHOTO)

As their numbers began to rebuild, gray whales became the quarry of early twentieth-century whalers, but success was minimal compared to that of the late 1800s.

Several nations involved in Pacific-coast whaling gave gray whales partial protection in 1937. Then, in 1946, under the International Convention for the Regulation of Whaling, fourteen countries agreed to halt the commercial exploitation of California gray whales. Today the United States is considering their removal from its endangered-species list, a proposition that has raised the ire of conservationists around the world.

"The government feels the eastern Pacific gray whale should be a candidate, an example of the first large cetacean that's been endangered, that has recovered under protection, and should be removed from the list of endangered and threatened species," says Dr. Steve Swartz, of the U.S. National Marine Fisheries Service. "This population, because it's recovered the way it has, is going to teach a lot about not only what whales do, but what they can't do, and what as managers we can and cannot accomplish. They're a good precedent-setting case, both in a biological sense and from a management perspective."

* * *

As with other great whales and marine mammals, the story of the gray whale's decrement is one of ignorance and greed. All of the gray whales in the Atlantic were wiped out in the seventeenth century. Few, if any, remain on the Asian side of the Pacific. Today the only healthy populations of gray whales are found along the Pacific coast of North America.

Yet these eastern Pacific gray whales came perilously close to the same fate as the grays of the Atlantic and Asia. Nowhere within their entire range could they find refuge from the assiduous whalers: they were massacred in the calving lagoons, harpooned on the migration route, and slaughtered in their feeding waters. No one knows how many were left before the collapse of the whaling industry—some say as few as two thousand, others say five thousand or more—but it was certainly a fraction of traditional numbers.

Gray whales were largely ignored by early whalers. Their baleen plates, the "plastic of the nineteenth-century," were too small; their oil was less plentiful and inferior to that of other whales, and the meat wasn't especially good. Compared to offshore species such as sperm whales, fins, blues, right whales, seis, and others, gray whales were hardly worth the effort—unless they could be taken in large quantities.

That opportunity arose in the mid-1800s when whalers scouting Mexican shores discovered three lagoons and a large bay used by wintering whales. In these shallow havens, where mothers serenely nurse their newborn offspring, where promiscuous gams of grays copulate in the subtropical sun, whales could be slain by the hundreds. Whaling "between the seasons," or "lagoon whaling," as it was known, began in earnest.

All four calving areas on the west coast of Baja California were targeted. The first was Magdalena Bay, eleven hundred kilometres down the coast from the U.S.-Mexico border. Here, where a string of islands protects the bay from the open sea, an estimated five hundred were killed between 1845 and '48. These seemingly docile animals soon earned the nicknames "hard head" or "devilfish" because of the way enraged females aggressively defended their young. Some whalers used that defensiveness to their advantage, harpooning calves to entice mothers within "darting distance." But before the end of the 1840s too many boats had been demolished by whales, too many men lost and seriously injured. Magdalena Bay was abandoned.

The desistance, however, was temporary. Sperm whales, the preferred prey, were being overfished. Baja was conveniently close to the major supply ports of San Francisco and Hawaii. Equipment and techniques were also improving. The Greener's harpoon gun, a swivel-mounted weapon fired from the bow of a ship, was becoming standard gear. The bomb-lance, which obliterated the internal organs of a whale, was fired from the shoulder like a musket. These items of destruction were used independently or in conjunction with one another. Often a harpoon was fired to attach a line to the whale, then the fleeing animal was killed with the explosive lance.

So the carnage continued: between 1854 and '65 at least another fifteen hundred grays were butchered at Magdalena Bay. During the same period, whalers began sailing their ships into Baja's three lagoon complexes. In the winter of 1859 and '60, Captain Charles Scammon took nearly four hundred whales from San Ignacio Lagoon, 250 kilometres north of Magdalena. He'd killed more than six hundred the previous year at Laguna Ojo de Liebre, known now as Scammon's Lagoon, 300 kilometres up the coast from San Ignacio. More whales were caught in Guerrero Negro, or Black Warrior Lagoon, which adjoins Scammon's Lagoon.

Entering the lagoons requires skillful navigation, and a few ships became casualties of poor judgement. Over the centuries, tides and prevailing winds have deposited sand

TINY SHRIMPLIKE EUPHAUSIIDS ARE AMONG THE PREY SOUGHT BY ENORMOUS GRAY WHALES. THESE PLANKTONIC CRUSTACEANS ARE THE MAINSTAY FOR A MULTITUDE OF MARINE ANIMALS, FROM HERRING AND SMALL SALMON, TO SEABIRDS AND GREAT WHALES. BY DEVOURING TONNES OF EUPHAUSIIDS AND OTHER MINUTE CREATURES, A GRAY WHALE MAY GROW TO THIRTY-ONE TONNES IN EIGHT OR TEN YEARS.

at the mouths of the lagoons, forming barrier islands that shelter the entrances from pounding Pacific surf. Strong tidal flows continuously scour deep, narrow channels leading into the lagoons behind the islands. Groves of tangled mangroves grow along some shorelines, but much of the land is desolate, a desert of rocks, sand, mud, and scrub. These lagoons support a prolificacy of marine life: they are spawning and rearing waters for fish; the fish attract dolphins, sharks, and a plethora of seabirds.

Before the whalers' arrival, the whales here had enjoyed an unmolested existence for a hundred millennia or more. Then, within three decades, the once bountiful calving waters held little attraction for whalers "between the seasons."

It was a self-defeating success, achieved at heavy human expense. "Hardly a day passes but there is upsetting or staving of boats, the crews receiving bruises, cuts, and, in many instances, having limbs broken; and repeated accidents have happened in which men have been instantly killed, or received mortal injury," Captain Scammon wrote in 1874.

Hunting on the open sea, where a harpooned whale had room to run, was significantly less hazardous. "But in a lagoon, the object of pursuit is in narrow passages, where frequently there is a swift tide, and the turbid water prevents the whaler from seeing far beneath the boat," Scammon wrote. "Should the chase be made with the current, the fugitive sometimes stops suddenly, and the speed of the boat, together with the influence of the running water, shoots it upon the worried animal when it is dashing its flukes in every direction. The whales that are chased have with them their young cubs, and the mother, in her efforts to avoid the pursuit of herself and offspring, may momentarily lose sight of her little one. Instantly she will stop and 'sweep' around in search, and if the boat comes in contact with her, it is quite sure to be staved. Another danger is, that in darting the lance at the mother, the young one, in its gambols, will get in the way of the weapon, and receive the wound, instead of the intended victim. In such instances, the parent animal, in her frenzy, will chase the boats, and, overtaking them, will overturn them with her head, or dash them in pieces with a stroke of her ponderous flukes."

It wasn't the perils, however, that turned the whalers away from the lagoons of Baja California. From the mid-1860s to the early '70s only 165 whales were taken from Magdalena Bay; San Ignacio yielded 55, and 42 were killed at Scammon's Lagoon.

Devastating as it was, lagoon whaling was only partly to blame for the gray whale's decline. Outside the lagoons, ships that anchored in bays around Vizcaino Peninsula attacked migrating whales. "Alongshore" whalers here killed nearly 1,000 gray whales while lagoon whaling was in its heyday. Another 165 were taken from the Gulf of California, on the opposite side of Baja.

During this same period, whaling stations were being established along the coast

YOUNG JASON ELLIS IS GREETED BY A CURIOUS GRAY WHALE NEAR TOFINO. THESE SO-CALLED "FRIENDLY" WHALES WERE FIRST DOCUMENTED IN 1975 WHEN WHALE-WATCHERS WERE AP-PROACHED AT SAN IGNACIO LA-GOON. IT WASN'T UNTIL THE EARLY 1980S THAT FRIENDLIES WERE ENCOUNTERED IN VAN-COUVER ISLAND WATERS. (JOHN FORD PHOTO) of Mexico and California. "Shore whalers" would launch small vessels to hunt whales migrating within about fifteen kilometres of the stations. Humpbacks and grays were most plentiful in near-shore waters and, because they migrated at different times, stations could operate up to eight months of the year. Many were manned by Portuguese immigrants from the Azores and Cape Verde islands. As they had done in their homelands, they went whaling during the seasons and farmed in the off-seasons.

After the first shore station was established in 1854 at Monterey Bay, others were soon to follow. Bolinas Bay, Santa Cruz, San Simeon, Point Conception, San Pedro, San Diego—a total of eighteen between Crescent City, California, and Punta Eugenia, Mexico. Records from shore stations often failed to differentiate between humpbacks and grays, so accurate catch figures for either species aren't available. But it's estimated that shore whalers killed at least twenty-five hundred gray whales between 1854 and 1874. Without large ships and sizeable crews to maintain, shore whaling was comparatively cheap. Even in the face of plummeting whale numbers, shore whalers continued to reap profits through the turn of the century. But by 1901 they too found few animals to process.

Whalers on the northern feeding grounds didn't enjoy the prosperity of whale hunters in southern waters. In the days when lagoon whaling was at its peak, northern whalers probably took fewer than 250 gray whales.

According to Scammon, other, less sophisticated whalers were also familiar with the gray whale's migratory habits. "Scarcely have the poor creatures quitted their southern homes before they are surprised by the Indians about the Strait of Juan de Fuca, Vancouver and Queen Charlotte's Islands. Like enemies in ambush, these glide in canoes from island, bluff, or bay, rushing upon their prey with whoop and yell, launching their instruments of torture, and like hounds worrying the last life-blood from their vitals."

Native whale hunts were immersed in ritual, and log books from early trading vessels suggest the Indians of Ahousat, off the west coast of Vancouver Island, customarily sacrificed a slave in honour of the first whale killed in a season. Whalers would bathe every night during the waxing of eight moons. Their bodies were rubbed with nettles and they swam in the sea, blowing and diving like whales, then floating on the surface, a dramatization of what they hoped their intended victims would do.

Fleets of two, four, up to six canoes, with crews of six to eight men stayed at sea as long as four or five days. Several seal-skin floats were attached to a harpoon by long lines of cedar bark and sinew. The chief, though not necessarily the most proficient whaler, made the first strike. The harpoon was thrown from a distance of one or two metres and the whale, taking refuge in the depths, fought against the buoyancy of the floats until exhausted.

A PACIFIC GRAY WHALE FIRES A HEART-SHAPED PLUME FROM ITS BLOWHOLES AS IT SURFACES OFF THE WEST COAST OF VANCOUVER ISLAND. ON STILL DAYS A BLOW MAY BE HEARD A KILOMETRE AWAY AS THE VAPOUR SHOOTS AS HIGH AS FIVE METRES ABOVE THE WHALE. (JOHN FORD PHOTO)

"The worried creature may dive deeply, but very little time elapses before the inflated seal-skins are visible again," Scammon wrote. "The instant these are seen, a buoy is elevated on a pole from the nearest canoe, by way of signal; then all dash, with shout and grunt, toward the object of pursuit. Now the chase attains the highest pitch of excitement, for each boat being provided with implements alike, in order to entitle it to a full share of the prize its crew must lodge their harpoon in the animal, with buoys attached; so that, after the first attack is made, the strife that ensues to be next to throw the spear creates a scene of brawl and agility peculiar to these savage adventurers. At length the victim, becoming weakened by loss of blood, yields to a system of torture characteristic of its eager pursuers, and eventually, spouting its last blood from a lacerated heart, it writhes in convulsions and expires."

Immediately after a kill the whale's mouth was tied shut to prevent it sinking. One crewman dived in, cut holes through the jaw and upper lip, slipped a line through, and cinched it tight. With seal-skin buoys to keep it afloat, the whale was towed ashore. Blubber was cut into strips and eaten. Some natives rendered blubber into oil by boiling it in long wooden tubs heated by hot stones. The amount of oil possessed by a chief was an indication of his wealth and he often traded his oil, like currency, with other Indians and early-day European explorers. Bones were used to make combs, clubs, or roof supports for buildings.

Farther north, Alaskan aborigines hunted alone or in pairs from bidarkas, or kayaks. Some anthropologists believe they laced their slate-tipped harpoons with aconite, a poison from a plant called monkshood. Unlike southern natives, they did not haul the whales home, but left the carcasses to drift ashore.

Aboriginal people hunted gray whales along the coast from central Washington to the Beaufort Sea. In spite of their diligence, hunts were often fraught with frustration. One report says that Maquinna, a powerful Vancouver Island chief in the late 1700s, spent a total of fifty-three days at sea one season: he struck and lost eight whales and landed one. Yet middens along the coast lie as mute testimony of the natives' success. An archaeological site with cetacean remains at Namu, on the central British Columbia coast, is about nine thousand years old. Another at Chaluka, in the Aleutian Islands, dates back about thirty-two hundred years, while one at Yuquot, on the west coast of Vancouver Island, is about three thousand years old.

Though whales were important to these natives, the effect of their hunting was insignificant compared to that of the whaling industry. By 1874 coastal aborigines, like the whales, had become victims of commercial whalers: gray whales, once such an integral part of native societies, were a rarity. Perhaps half, maybe more, of North America's entire

A DEAD WHALE EXPOSES A GREY AREA IN CANADIAN LAW. FEDERAL FISHERIES AUTHORITIES ARE RESPONSIBLE ONLY FOR LIVE WHALES. THE COAST GUARD HANDLES NAVIGATIONAL HAZARDS, BUT THIS ANIMAL IS NO LONGER FLOATING, AND IT'S TOO LARGE FOR THE LOCAL SPCA. THIS ANIMAL, WASHED UP NEAR VANCOUVER'S STANLEY PARK, WAS TEMPORARILY MOORED IN SAANICH INLET BEFORE IT WAS TOWED BY FISHERIES OFFICIALS TO THE WEST COAST OF VANCOUVER ISLAND AND SUNK WITH EIGHT WHEELS FROM A RAILCAR. (JOHN FORD PHOTO)

Pacific gray-whale population was annihilated between 1845 and 1874: eight thousand whales, possibly ten thousand—nobody is sure.

The future for the California gray may not have been so bleak if numbers were all that mattered. But this fishery had concentrated largely on adult cows, eliminating a huge segment of the population's prime producers. The killing of thousands of lactating females also caused the deaths of offspring they were nursing. And the potential, the calves those cows would have borne every second year, was also gone. It would take many generations to recover.

It seems ironic that Captain Scammon, whose hands were soiled by the blood of innumerable gray whales, appeared remorseful in his writings. "The large bays and lagoons, where these animals once congregated, brought forth and nurtured their young, are already nearly deserted. The mammoth bones of the California Gray lie bleaching on the shores of those silvery waters, and are scattered along the broken coasts, from Siberia to the Gulf of California; and ere it may be questioned whether this mammal will not be numbered among the extinct species of the Pacific."

Fortunately, Scammon's prediction was proven false. Gray whales enjoyed a four-decade reprieve from hunters, long enough to noticeably improve the stocks. After 1910, steam whalers from Norway, Japan, Russia, and United States reappeared along North America's Pacific shores to once again take gray whales. Before they were protected in 1946, nearly a thousand more whales were taken from the slowly rebuilding population.

The treaty which banned the commercial killing of gray whales allowed Russian whalers to take about two hundred a year for use by Soviet aborigines. It also permitted "scientific collections": in 1953 Canadians killed ten gray whales for research; Americans took 316 between 1959 and 1970. Further protection was given in 1972, when Laguna Guerrero Negro and Scammon's Lagoon were declared the world's first gray-whale sanctuaries. The Mexican government extended the same status to Laguna San Ignacio in 1979.

* * *

One of the last scientific collections was Gigi, a female calf borrowed from the wild, held at San Diego Sea World for a year, and released. On March 13, 1971, at Scammon's Lagoon, she was caught by the tail with a noose affixed to the end of a long pole. After a three-day cruise the young whale was put in a two-hundred-thousand-litre tank and fed through a tube inserted in her throat.

When Gigi arrived she weighed 1,950 kilograms and measured nearly six metres long. Having been seized from her mother at the age of two months, the whale was not enamoured with her captors. She acted violently toward anyone trying to take her temperature, her pulse, or blood samples. She refused to eat for two weeks, losing sixty-

A GRAY WHALE'S MOST FORMID- ABLE FOE IS THE KILLER WHALE. WHILE YOUNG CALVES ARE MOST VULNERABLE, ADULT GRAYS THAT SURVIVE ORCA ATTACKS ARE FREQUENTLY LEFT WITH PERMA- NENT TEETH MARKS SCARRED ON THEIR SKIN. (JOHN FORD PHOTO)

eight kilos. Finally she accepted a formula of ground squid and bonito, cod liver oil, brewer's yeast, vitamins, corn oil, whipping cream, and water. As her appetite improved, she was weaned onto nine-kilogram blocks of frozen squid—she ate a hundred a day.

Before long Gigi was gaining eleven kilograms a day. By the end of May she weighed twenty-five hundred kilos. By November she was up to thirty-eight hundred kilograms and measured more than seven metres from head to tail. When she was released, one year to the day from her capture, she weighed six thousand kilograms and was eight metres long.

While at Sea World, Gigi was moved to a larger tank for public display. Scientists monitored her growth, studied her eating habits, recorded her sounds, and conducted various tests. Before her release Gigi was cryogenically "branded" with a large square behind the blowhole. A radio transmitter was surgically implanted in her blubber with four stainless steel sutures.

On the morning of March 13, 1972, she was barged out to the gray-whale migration route, about eight kilometres west of San Diego, and set free. Immediately she uttered a long series of clicks, similar to those emitted by gray whales feeding at Vancouver Island's Wickaninnish Bay. She issued more than thirteen hundred clicks in four minutes, baffling scientists who hadn't heard the sounds during her captivity.

Unafraid of people, the curious young whale approached bathers at Dana Point, between San Diego and Los Angeles. She surfaced and blew, sending swimmers scrambling for shore. Apparently Gigi cleared three beaches as she wandered up the coast. Her radio transmitter beeped for the last time near Monterey Bay on May 5, indicating she'd joined the northbound migration. It wasn't until December, 1977, that Gigi was identified again: a boater off San Diego's Point Loma patted and stroked her while someone took pictures. Since 1979, when she was seen at San Ignacio Lagoon with a new calf, Gigi has been spotted several times.

* * *

The Pacific gray-whale population in the eastern Pacific was probably thirteen or fourteen thousand in 1977 when Steve Swartz and his partner, Mary Lou Jones, began their research at San Ignacio Lagoon. Their interest in gray whales developed not long after their interest in each other.

Swartz, who'd grown up in the San Fernando Valley, earned a bachelor's degree from the University of California at Santa Barbara. After six years of odd-jobbing he returned to university to work towards a master's degree in ichthyology, but jobs in the fish field were scarce, so he took a position in San Diego teaching students who visited Sea World.

It was the early 1970s, the days when the star attractions at oceanariums were pretty

"sea maids" bucking about on the backs of whales and dolphins. Mary Lou Jones, also a native of southern California, was one of Sea World's performing trainers. Like her future husband, she too held a bachelor's degree.

As members of the American Cetacean Society, Jones and Swartz were regular volunteers for the annual winter gray-whale count off San Diego. "We wanted to know what was going on in Mexico so we made a short trip down there, Mary Lou and I, and saw what was happening," says Swartz. "We became really excited about it." Little study had been done on the activities of gray whales in calving lagoons, and Jones and Swartz determined at least five winters would be needed to compile an adequate data base. The U.S. government was also concerned about the effects of whale-watchers who travelled down the coast from San Diego to observe mating grays.

San Ignacio, the most southerly of the calving lagoons, is a near-pristine inland sea surrounded by desert. It is inhabited by about six hundred whales at the peak of the season, and is small enough—about 160 square kilometres—to be surveyed by boat in a day.

"We wanted to look at whales without the influence of humans around, with the exception of whale-watching, which happened sporadically and in a specific area within the lagoon," says Swartz. They formed Cetacean Research Associates and, with backing from the Marine Mammal Commission, World Wildlife Fund, National Geographic Society, and others, Jones and Swartz began the research that would carry them into the next decade.

From a research perspective, studying whales in a remote setting, free of human disturbance, is appealing. Logistically, it's not without its headaches. Each winter from

1977 to '82 Jones, Swartz, and their assistants loaded their Volkswagen bus and other assorted vehicles and left for San Ignacio between Christmas and New Year's, prepared to stay until mid-April. The team usually consisted of four or five researchers, but at times as many as a dozen occupied the camp. They needed shelter, food and supplies, boat gas, and drinking water—precious commodities in the middle of a seaside desert.

Civilization was the town of San Ignacio, population two thousand, an oasis of lush palms and citrus orchards in a valley where the vast Vizcaino Desert meets the foothills of Baja's eastern mountains. Eight kilometres by boat, eighty kilometres across the desert on a Jeep track that was there, or not there, depending on recent rains: a one-way trip to town varied between four hours and all day.

They developed a "reciprocal relationship" with the whale-watching industry. "We sent back empty Igloo ice chests," says Swartz. "Our friends would meet them when they reached port in San Diego and trade them for full Igloo ice chests. We'd send up frantic shopping lists of things that broke, or needed replacement or repair, and they would send things back down. In return we gave natural history talks to the passengers. . . . And we paid them a flat shipping fee each year to carry freight back and forth for us. That way we could get fresh water and produce on a regular basis, and every once in a while some ice cream."

Though periodically dampened by storms, San Ignacio is usually bathed in glorious subtropical sun. The searing temperatures common to these southern climes are chilled here by cold upwelling Pacific waters, bringing balmy, even cool, breezes from the open sea, along with occasional fog.

Home for three and a half months was Punta Piedra—Rocky Point—a tiny peninsula near the mouth of the lagoon. "It was surrounded on three sides by impenetrable mangrove estuary, so you were, in fact, on an island. We'd set up a little tent city. You couldn't build any permanent structures because it's difficult to get wood down there and there's none to be found. So we put up tents. They worked fine except when the wind blew hard and the rain came down at the same time: then they all blew down. . . . Our camp was blown down routinely a couple of times a year. If it happened in the middle of the night it was rather irritating. We had a Super Cub there one season and it tried to fly by itself. We had to chain it to the ground."

Chubascos—pitiless, Mexican storms with dark, spongy clouds—would surge up the coast and sweep across the lagoon. "Whenever the wind came up from the south we'd get nervous. We knew we were going to use up all our garbage bags wrapping everything to keep it dry because inevitably it was going to rain, and it always rained heavily. The desert is so flat: there's no runoff and the shores were a composite of sand and a kind

BONY BALEEN PLATES, SIMILAR IN COMPOSITION TO THE HUMAN FINGERNAIL, HANG FROM THE UPPER JAW OF A GRAY WHALE. THE OUTER EDGES ARE SMOOTH, WHILE THE INNER EDGES ARE LINED WITH BRISTLES OR FIBRES. THE WHALE SUCKS IN HUGE QUANTITIES OF SAND, WATER, AND FOOD, THEN EXPELS IT THROUGH THE BALEEN WITH THE FORCE OF A FOURTEEN-HUNDRED-KILOGRAM TONGUE, CATCHING EUPHAUSIIDS, TUBE-WORMS, AMPHIPODS, AND OTHER MINUTE MARINE CREATURES. (JOHN FORD PHOTO)

of clay, silt, and it would just turn to mush." Sometimes they'd wait out storms for five or six days, reading, playing guitar, or wandering about the desert.

They couldn't wander far afield without risking the pilferages of plunderous ravens. Most desert animals—coyotes, badgers, rattlesnakes—kept a wary distance, but the ravens would strut right into camp and help themselves.

"They keyed into our garbage immediately and began to scatter it every time we turned our backs," Swartz recalls. "So we had to go through these elaborate procedures to raven-proof the camp. We'd go away for a couple of hours and come back and think that somebody had looted us. They work in pairs and these two birds would undo everything. They'd turn over stoves, empty trash bins, tear open bags, and scatter things around. They were quite hilarious; we got a real kick out of the ravens."

Wildlife, besides whales, was among San Ignacio's enticements for Jones and Swartz. Their bird records list more than 150 species, from kingfishers to loons, sandpipers, and ducks. Coyote-free islands in the upper reaches of the lagoon are nesting grounds for ospreys, pelicans, cormorants, and a multitude of seabirds. The fish that feed these avian visitors provided many meals for the researchers.

There was one instance when a researcher nearly provided a meal for a fish. Jones was bathing near camp, splashing about like a sea otter in chest-deep water. She turned around to look into the sunset and as the water cleared from her eyes they focused on a dorsal fin headed her way. 'Ah, a bottlenose dolphin's coming to play,' she figured. But the dorsal fin, straight and stable, was followed by a tail fin, zigzagging sinuously along the surface.

"The long and short of it is she got out of the water and screamed," Swartz recalls. "I ran over there and this shark, which turned out to be about a twelve-foot hammerhead, spent about fifteen minutes cruising around looking for her, thrashing the water, swimming, until it finally gave up and left." The shark had come within two metres of its intended meal. "It was pretty scary. After that we all took baths together, or at least in teams of two, someone sitting up on the rocks watching while the other person splashed around."

The procession of whales past Punta Piedra was watched from a five-metre viewing tower, built of aluminum tubing by an engineer friend. The platform, a four-by-eight sheet of plywood, was enclosed by knee-high walls. "We had sort of a playpen up there, to keep us from falling out in moments of exaltation when you think you've seen something really neat." The rig looked like an oil derrick anchored to the ground with guy wires.

While the Swartz-Jones team set up camp, the first wintering whales returned. Some would stay a few days then leave; others would remain in the lagoon until spring. By late January and early February, whales were migrating in both directions: the last to leave

WHO'S CURIOUS, THE WHALE OR THE WHALE WATCHER? ALTHOUGH WHALE-WATCHING APPEARS TO HAVE NO EFFECT ON GRAY WHALES IN MEXICAN CALVING WATERS, IN RECENT YEARS SOME GRAYS MIGRATING ALONG THE COAST OF SOUTHERN CALIFORNIA HAVE ABANDONED TRADITIONAL NEAR-SHORE TRAVEL ROUTES. RESEARCHERS ATTRIBUTE THE BEHAVIOURAL CHANGE NOT TO THE GROWING WHALE-WATCHING INDUSTRY, BUT TO AN OVERALL INCREASE IN MARINE TRAFFIC. (STEVE SWARTZ PHOTO) the Bering and Chukchi seas were just arriving at the lagoon, while the early northbound migrants were already starting to move back up the coast.

"They don't all go into a lagoon and sit there for the winter," Swartz explains. "It's a real dynamic system." By mid-season a steady two-way stream of whales is flowing through the mouth of the lagoon, as many as 500 a day. In one seven-hour survey, while there were 270 whales in the lagoon, at least 341 entered and 185 left.

With all this coming and going, there must be a great deal of activity outside the lagoon. But for scientists in a small skiff, the entrance is foreboding, with breakers foaming over the sandbars and tides racing through the narrow channels. They'd navigated the gateway in large vessels but not in the inflatable Zodiac, so they'd never had a close look outside. One day, after a series of storms, their curiosity got the better of them.

"It was gorgeous," Swartz remembers. "You know the feeling you get after a storm: the sky is clear, the sun is bright and sparkling, the water's oily smooth. We cut the engine

and you could hear this low, rumbled roar. The whole scene was so surrealistic: big white combers are breaking over to the west, and we're sitting on the inside on this slick, green, satiny carpet. It was slack tide; we all looked at each other and said, 'Yeah, we're going for it.'

"Once we were out there we could see this big ground swell coming in. By the time the ground swell peaked up and curled, it was probably twelve feet, maybe fifteen feet tall from the trough to the crest. Lo and behold a whale would come splitting down the middle of a big comber, surfing like a huge redwood log. They'd be kicking for all they were worth, and they'd ride the swells in. Then when the wave would break onto the shallow bar; they'd just come rolling up, turn around, and splash their way back out again.

"They were having a great time. It was just one of those magical experiences. Everything was perfect and the whales caught us totally by surprise. We'd never have known they did that unless we'd gone out there and watched."

Back inside, the Zodiac was used to run transects of the lagoon. A team of at least four was needed for surveys—one to operate the boat, two to watch, photograph and record the whales' behaviour, and one to remain at camp near the radio. "We were out on the water in a remote area and there were sharks in the lagoon. So whenever there was a boat crew out, there was always somebody within earshot of the radio. If there was a problem, at least you might get word of it. There's no sense having a radio if you don't use it."

Their pioneering spirit was put to the test when they found they'd have to produce their own hydrographic chart: the only existing map of the lagoon was a century old. Local fishermen viewed them with justified skepticism when they repeatedly, and intentionally, ran their boat aground on sandbars, then noted their positions on the ancient chart. The lagoon boundaries were delineated by satellite imagery; the seafloor contours were mapped with fathometer recordings. Once the fishermen discovered what these strangers were up to, they were keen to offer suggestions for Spanish place names.

Many of the fishermen are among a half-dozen families who live around the lagoon, harvesting fish—including sharks in the forty- to ninety-kilogram range—and raising cattle on the uplands. Like the researchers, they carry citizens' band radios and are reliable allies in an emergency.

"We developed a working relationship with our neighbours," says Swartz. "The first couple of years they thought we were just tourists. By the third year they thought we were absolutely crazy to keep coming back. By the fourth year we were having regular volleyball games, having dinner at their ranches once in a while. We kind of got integrated; in fact, we still get Christmas cards."

With the lagoon charted and the viewing tower in place, the research was well under way. From the beginning, the photo-identification of individual whales was an integral aspect of the studies. Jim Darling, a Canadian gray-whale expert, had been photographing whales off Vancouver Island since the early 1970s. He had found, as Mike Bigg had found with orcas, that gray whales too have distinctive markings, such as scars and scratches or variations in pigmentation. Darling came to San Ignacio at the outset of the first field season and taught Jones and Swartz how to photo-identify whales. Eventually, with more than six thousand photographs, the identification of over four hundred whales allowed the researchers to determine breeding frequency of specific females, the time certain animals spend at San Ignacio, and circulation of whales both inside and outside the lagoon.

Photo-identification helped Jones deduce that 81 percent of courting whales stay in the lagoon for a week or less. It is nonetheless a hectic week for amorous whales. The mouth of the lagoon, below the viewing tower, is a popular mating site. From their observation point, Jones and Swartz could see that the breeding of gray whales is a sexual free-for-all which surely must guarantee the perpetuity of the species: with groups of ten, twenty, thirty or more whales unabashedly sharing partners, some animals are sure to get pregnant.

During "mating bouts" of up to four hours, females have intercourse with several males. Partners lie belly-to-belly in shallow water, copulating for a few minutes, climaxing, as one researcher puts it, "with a massive orgasmic shudder." The duration of the carnality appears to be decided by the female, who rejects the advances of her suitors by fleeing or lying upside-down on the surface. With most gray-whale cows producing a calf every second year, only half the female population is available for breeding. Despite the shortage of cows, there is no rivalry or aggression among mating bulls vying for the affections of estrous females.

A RESEARCH TEAM'S TENT SITS BELOW A FIVE-METRE VIEWING TOWER AT PUNTA PIEDRA, NEAR THE ENTRANCE TO SAN IGNACIO LAGOON. DURING ONE SEVEN-HOUR STINT IN THE TOWER, OBSERVERS WATCHED AT LEAST 341 WHALES ENTER THE LAGOON AND 185 LEAVE. (STEVE SWARTZ PHOTO)

After gestations of twelve months, births occur from late December to early March, with most in late January. Cows with newborns avoid the mating scene, moving into the "nursery," the upper reaches of the lagoon where the depth averages four or five metres. By February as many as a hundred cow-calf pairs are sharing these waters, resting, nursing, and swimming with the tides.

As part of her work for a master's thesis, Jones was attempting to define the advantages of calving lagoons for gray whales. While doing census work during the southward migration in California's Channel Islands National Marine Sanctuary, she was surprised to discover newborn calves eight hundred kilometres north of the nearest calving lagoon. "They were born at the right time, but they weren't where we thought they ought to be, which is farther south," says Jones. "They had to be born there; they were so small, definitely newborn animals. So a number of questions are raised. Is there a survival advantage to being born farther south? Do calves born during the southward migration do just as well as those born down in Mexico?"

During an aerial survey over the Channel Islands, in the Southern California Bight, Jones and Swartz watched an orca kill a gray-whale calf. After witnessing the attack, they surmised that the lagoons likely provide safety in numbers. "Although the lagoons are packed with gray whales, orcas have never been observed inside. Perhaps the predation rate is a lot less if you move into a shallow-water area with a bunch of your buddies around," says Swartz. "You'll be a lot less vulnerable than out in open water, going through those deep channels, island hopping. They're definitely vulnerable, especially going slow with a new calf that has to stay near the surface."

Newborn calves are tiny, by gray-whale standards: a mere four or five metres long, weighing seven hundred to nine hundred kilograms. Feeding on milk containing 53-percent fat—one of the richest in the world—a calf may grow another metre and double its birth weight by the time it leaves the lagoon. When it is weaned at seven or eight months it will likely measure nine metres long and weigh six or seven thousand kilograms. When sexually mature, at about eight years old, a female may measure thirteen metres and weigh thirty-one thousand kilos; a male could be twelve metres and weigh as much as twenty-six thousand kilograms. Like orcas, they are long-lived cetaceans: it's believed some reach sixty or eighty years of age.

Although mother gray whales abandon their young within a year of birth, the bond between cows and newborns is strong. "While playing, the little ones often climb all over their resting mothers," Jones and Swartz write in an *Oceans* magazine article. "They swim onto her rotund back and slide off, roll across her massive tail stock, and pummel her with their leaping back-flops and belly-flops. Mothers appear very tolerant of all this and frequently join in, repeatedly lifting the calf out of the water, whereupon the calf flails itself back down with a splash. Calves also appear to frolic in Jacuzzi-like 'bubble-bursts' created when their mothers release explosions of air underwater which boil to the surface."

Photo-identification shows that some cows return to the same lagoon each year. Others may bear a calf in one lagoon, then choose a different lagoon two years later. Some cow-calf pairs move among two or three calving areas within the same season. When the mating whales have gone in spring, cows and calves congregate near the mouth of the lagoon. San Ignacio appears to be a staging area where cows with calves gather before heading north. Many from Magdalena Bay stop at San Ignacio on their northbound migrations. Surprisingly, some pairs from Guerrero Negro and Scammon's lagoons travel down the coast for three hundred kilometres to San Ignacio, where they join other whales preparing to swim north in March or April.

Jones and Swartz watched calves gaining strength by swimming against strong tides in mid-channel, going nowhere. During this pre-migration training, youngsters become more explorative, taking short stints away from their mothers. Groups of a dozen pairs rollick in the afternoon sun, obviously enjoying one another's company.

THE MATING OF GRAY WHALES IS A SEXUAL FREE-FOR-ALL IN WHICH GROUPS OF TEN, TWENTY, THIRTY OR MORE UNABASHEDLY SHARE PARTNERS. RESEARCHERS SAY THAT 81 PERCENT OF COURTING WHALES STAY AT SAN IGNACIO LAGOON FOR ONE WEEK OR LESS. (STEVE SWARTZ PHOTO)

"People have this concept that toothed whales, dolphins, are the only social cetaceans," says Swartz. "We saw groups of female gray whales with calves congregating and all we can describe is a social type of interaction. The calves run around chasing each other, playing, and the females loll around, splashing and jumping. At a distance, because of the splashing and commotion, you'd think you had a mating group. But when you got out there and started looking at everybody, you'd find they were all females and they all had calves."

In an article for *National Geographic*, Jones and Swartz describe an incident which demonstrates both the social and protective nature of mother gray whales. "From our observation tower on Punta Piedra next to a deep channel, we saw a calf thrashing as it left the channel and tried to cross a shallow sandbar.

"Instantly, an adult whale we took to be the calf's mother surged out of the channel and beached itself beside the calf. Seconds later another whale beached itself on the other side, sandwiching the calf between two adults. Both adults thereupon raised their heads and flukes, pivoted with the calf between them, and slid smoothly back into the channel."

"In itself, the incident was impressive," says Jones, "but we were really impressed when the same thing happened a second time in the same place one year later."

The playful activity at the mouth of the lagoon suggests that gray whales have a communication system, although it's unlikely they use echolocation or sophisticated dialects like killer whales. "But they do use sounds," says Swartz. "For example, if a female wants to recall her calf from a group of calves, or if she's sleeping and decides to leave, she utters some sort of sound. The calf responds immediately and off they go. So there's definitely communication going on amongst them. Exactly how it's carried out and what's the significance under various circumstances I don't know. No one's done the definitive work on the gray whale's song, if you will, or on gray whale dialects."

Scientists who analyzed eighteen thousand metres of recording tape in the late 1960s claimed that Pacific grays were among the most vocal of all whales. They described a variety of sounds, including clicks, rasps, and the "bong of a huge Chinese gong." Others say they've heard snorts, moans, grunts, low-pitched roars, metallic "blip blips" like percolating coffee, and the sound of a hammer against a wooden hull. Researchers at Scammon's Lagoon say the clicks are most often heard when a plane or helicopter passes closely overhead: perhaps they are an expression of anger or irritation. It's not uncommon for a gray whale to emit a series of quick clicks while trying to strike a hovering helicopter with its flukes.

In the early 1980s researcher Marilyn Dahlheim taped gray whales for two hundred hours at San Ignacio Lagoon. She defined seven distinct sounds and determined a number of situations in which the whales are most vocal—when grouped in a small area or when interacting with bottlenose dolphins; when on a collision course with a boat or another whale; when single whales are chasing cow-calf pairs; or when boat noise and other ambient sounds are prevalent. Other scientists learned that gray whales interpret sounds made by other cetaceans: when killer-whale calls were played near gray whales the grays immediately turned away and ran.

Dahlheim provided an important clue to the mysterious "friendly-whale phenomenon." She determined that noise from outboard motors occupies the same frequency as gray-whale sounds. Since whale-watching began at calving lagoons in the early 1970s, the number of so-called "friendlies" has increased significantly. These whales approach small craft, often rubbing alongside, bumping and blowing beneath the boats, allowing passengers to reach out and pat them. They invariably seek vessels with engines idling.

Swartz learned to use his outboard to elicit sounds from whales. "They generally approached it from underneath, or from behind, and pointed themselves right at the idling engine. We could actually get them to trumpet blow, like a humpback, by revving the outboard engine. They expel bubbles underwater and there's quite a bit of sound associated with those big bubble bursts. They'd blast, we'd rev the engine and they'd blast again. We'd get this kind of rapport going back and forth. But if we shut the engine off, the friendlies would leave the boat, abandon it."

In the North Pacific, only gray whales exhibit this apparent fondness for humans. Humpbacks in Hawaii often spy-hop beside tour boats; minke whales are known to bow ride. In 1991, after studying orcas for twenty-three years, Graeme Ellis patted a wild killer whale for the first time. But many gray whales seem to actually solicit the tender touch of the human hand. Whether it's simple curiosity or genuine friendliness is uncertain.

Jones and Swartz encountered friendly whales immediately after establishing themselves at San Ignacio. In their *National Geographic* article Jones quotes from her journal of February 15, 1977, recalling her first meeting with a friendly. "There, less than an arm's length away, above the gape of the mouth, was the large brown eye of the whale, staring directly back at me and following my every move." The whale was a female, about nine metres long and probably about two years old. She became known to whale watchers as Amazing Grace for her amazing friendliness and graceful movements.

"From our first encounter with Amazing Grace, she readily adopted us, along with our fourteen-foot inflatable outboard, as her personal toys. She would roll under the boat, turn belly up with her flipper sticking three or four feet out of the water on either side of the craft, then lift us clear off the surface of the lagoon, perched high and dry on her chest between her massive flippers.

"When she tired of the bench-press technique, Grace would do the same thing with her head, lifting us out of the water and letting us slide off to swirl around her in circles, like a big rubber duck in the bathtub with a ten-ton playmate. At other times Grace would submerge beneath us and release a tremendous blast of air that boiled to the surface in a giant Jacuzzi of white water that engulfed us and the boat.

"After such gymnastics Grace would often lie quietly alongside the boat to be rubbed. We would oblige her with a vigorous massage along her back and head, while she opened her mouth to display huge fringed curtains of creamy white baleen plates."

Through the years a few curious whales that became familiar were given names—Peanut, Cabrillo, Haleakala, Pinto. "You notice that some of them have different personality traits that separate them from other whales," says Swartz. "There was one humongous whale we named Rosebud. She was as curious, as friendly as can be, but she wouldn't let us touch her. She'd come up to the boat and station herself there, but stay just out of reach for an hour. In the years when she had a calf she'd let the calf play with us for hours. We'd rub it, play with it, it'd bump the boat. Rosebud would just hang out, but not let us touch her."

A mischievous friendly named Bopper was one to avoid. "We didn't like to spend a lot of time with Bopper because Bopper got a real thrill out of coming up under the boat and giving it a good whack. Some of the tour boats' customers got a good fright. They soon got hip to Bopper because it would come over under the auspices of being a friendly, touchy-feely type, and all of a sudden this thing would lay into the boat and shake the people up."

People in four-metre boats should be wary of whales three times the length of their vessels, in spite of the animals' presumable friendliness. "They're big and they could quite easily do some damage inadvertently," Swartz warns. "We never had any aggressive encounters with them, but there were a couple of accidents in the time we were down there: people were cruising along and a whale came up underneath and a boat went over. No one was ever seriously hurt in San Ignacio, but there were a couple of deaths from a whale-watching incident like that in Scammon's Lagoon. Fortunately for us, there were just a few collisions that made everybody pay attention."

A few years after Jones and Swartz had completed their field work, an underwater cinematographer was almost killed by a gray whale. Howard Hall was delivered a pulverizing "karate chop" by a gray whale's most menacing weapon—150-kilogram flukes nearly four metres wide. He was having little success in filming mating whales in the turbid waters of San Ignacio when he ran across a trio of breeders, apparently moving towards his underwater position.

"Suddenly, great ominous shadows swirled all around me, and I knew that the huge creatures were almost upon me," Hall writes in *International Wildlife* magazine. "But there was no shape to the shadows. I squinted into the darkness for some hint of form, some idea of what to do, where to go. But there was no place to go. I switched on the camera and pointed it randomly in front of me.

"A moment later, a shadow darkened and transformed itself into a huge mountain of gray flesh. It was the face of a whale, and it was only six feet away. For a fraction of a second our eyes met. Adrenalin rushed through my system. In the eye of the whale I was certain I saw fear. There was a discernible tremor in its body.

"The whale quickly turned and accelerated away. For perhaps two seconds I was alone, but instinctively I knew that I was in great danger. I curled up in a ball and held the camera close to my chest. Then the impact came.

"Four things happened nearly simultaneously. I saw what looked like a shining semicircular white arch of light extending from in front of me to my left side—an arch I later determined was probably the vortex left behind as the flukes swung sideways. At my left side I caught the fleeting image of the flukes as they smashed into my body, edge on. In my head, I heard the sound of an explosion as if a shotgun had been fired in my ear. Then the lights went out."

Hall, semiconscious, struggled into his boat with the help of a friend. His mask and a glove were missing. Two ribs were broken and his left arm was fractured.

Whether by intention or inadvertence, wild gray whales can inflict serious injury on people who venture too close. But do people pose any threat to the whales? When Jones and Swartz examined the effects of whale-watching at San Ignacio, "friendlies" were a relatively new phenomenon. They caught tour operators off guard in the winter of 1975-76, the first season they were documented approaching boats and allowing passengers to pat them. They were still rare in the late 1970s, but by the early '80s encounters with friendly whales were becoming common.

In 1981 there were twenty-eight whale-watching excursions into the lagoon: twenty-six crossed paths with friendlies which allowed nearly seven hundred passengers to pat them. The next year people on thirty trips repeatedly interacted with friendly gray whales. It was happening in other lagoons and elsewhere in the gray whales' range. A researcher in the Bering Sea was followed for about twenty minutes in 1982. Boats off Vancouver Island in 1983 were approached many times by a curious gray whale.

Many whales of both sexes and all ages have become friendly. Sometimes they seem to attract one another, gathering in groups, following boats for long periods. They breach and tail-lob beside open skiffs, saturating passengers.

The growing number of friendlies suggests the animals are becoming accustomed to whale-watchers. Mothers who freely allow their calves to interact with people must not see humans as a threat. Jones and Swartz surmise that today's gray whales have never been harassed by whalers and are therefore not conditioned to avoid the advances of small skiffs.

The researchers concluded that the level of whale-watching in San Ignacio Lagoon has no adverse biological effect on the animals. The whales have not shifted away from the lagoon with the increase in tours: in fact the number of gray whales has steadily increased since whale-watching began in the early seventies.

Jones and Swartz attribute some of the increase to regulations enforced in the sanctuary. The middle and upper sections of the lagoon are off-limits to tour boats, providing an undisturbed area where newborns can gain strength and females may find solitude. Vessels with permits are allowed in the lower lagoon, yet they don't appear to bother the whales. This area consistently contains 65 percent of the single whales during the first half of each winter; it's later occupied by 87 percent of the cow-calf pairs.

The methods of tour operators also could be responsible for the harmonious relationship between human and animal. They want to provide a look at free-roaming whales; they know it's pointless to pursue them, that there's greater success in letting the whales run the show.

Lagoon tours are a minor component of the whale-watching industry compared to day-trips along the southern California migration corridors. Outside the lagoons the industry, with other marine traffic, is affecting the whales' habits. These operators recently have been forced to travel farther afield to satisfy their customers.

"The implication is that all of the boating activity, both commercial and recreational, has had some effect on the whales' use of the near-shore migratory route," Swartz explains. Between San Diego and Point Conception the whales traditionally fan out and use several routes through the Channel Islands, some near shore, some farther out to sea. "So they've always been using offshore corridors, but what appears to have happened is that in the last decade or so the animals are beginning to abandon routes in close to shore, within a mile or two."

Other perils face gray whales as they leave their southern asylums. To killer whales and sharks, gray whales are gourmet food; some calves become disoriented and separated from their mothers before being weaned. Jones and Swartz estimate that about 5.4 percent of the new calves die from various causes within the lagoons. Many that survive the winter in a lagoon aren't strong enough to withstand the rigours of open-sea travel. Thirty-one percent of the calves that begin the migration die before they reach southern California: over a third of each year's calves never make it beyond Mexican waters. Records from 1950 to 1981 show that calves comprised 43 percent of ninety-seven known gray-whale strandings along the migration route.

To track the movements of migrating whales, researchers Bruce Mate and James Harvey found some approachable grays at San Ignacio Lagoon and fitted them with radio transmitters. A total of eighteen were tagged between February and April in 1979 and '80. They were monitored by air and from shore-based receiving stations. One whale tagged on February 27, 1979, was beeping signals to La Jolla, California, forty-three days later. Within the next eighteen days it appeared off Newport, Oregon. Thirty-three days later it was swimming through Unimak Pass, Alaska. It had travelled nearly seven thousand kilometres in ninety-four days. Five researchers from the University of California saw the same whale twenty-seven months later.

The next year four cow-calf pairs and three single adults were relocated a total of sixteen times after they left San Ignacio. The tagging offered additional proof that gray whales move among breeding areas. After leaving San Ignacio one single female was located down in Magdalena Bay twenty-four days later. Within the next ten days her signals were picked up five hundred kilometres north of San Ignacio.

The distances covered by tagged animals varied from a few kilometres to well over 100 kilometres a day. Overall, they averaged 85 kilometres a day on the northbound migration. They picked up the pace in northern waters, swimming about 127 kilometres in each of the last twenty-nine days. They generally travelled slower on the northbound migration, averaging 88 kilometres a day from Piedras Blancas, south of Monterey, to Unimak Pass. When heading south they moved between Unimak Pass and Monterey at a speed of 125 kilometres a day.

Radio telemetry was later used to determine whether southbound gray whales travel the same speed at night as during the day. Population estimates were based on fifteen winter counts taken between 1967 and '86 from a shore station at Granite Canyon, near Monterey. During that time the number of whales was believed to have grown by about 2.5 percent a year from approximately eleven thousand to fifteen or sixteen thousand. But 58 percent of the total migration was interpolated from daylight figures—no one really knew how many whales passed in the night.

So Steve Swartz attached transmitters, encased in steel cylinders, to eighteen whales. A crossbow was used to fire each unit into the blubber of a whale, and barbs prevented it from dislodging. One would wonder how an animal sensitive to the touch of a human hand would react to metal barbs penetrating its skin, but tagged whales exhibited no signs of pain. The device was shot from the bowsprit of a boat when a whale surfaced below, allowing the antenna to stand upright. The animals were tagged from late morning to afternoon, then tracked overnight by boat or shore station until dawn or until they reached the end of a specific study area.

For two weeks in January, Swartz followed nine whales between Piedras Blancas and Monterey for 28 hours of daylight and 102 hours of darkness. Nine others were later tracked through the Channel Islands for 30 hours during the day, 26 hours at night.

The conclusion was that swimming speeds near the tail end of the southbound migration are the same, day or night: the whales average six kilometres an hour, twenty-four hours a day. Another whale mystery put to rest.

* * *

Up off the southwest coast of Vancouver Island the gray whales have arrived at Long Beach, as they do every year when the last days of winter surrender to spring. The Whale Festival is in full swing, and tourists crowd the shops of Tofino, a seaside village of a thousand just north of Pacific Rim National Park. They're procuring posters, buttons, carvings, T-shirts, postcards, and other west-coast paraphernalia. Down on the docks sightseers are boarding tour boats and heading for the open seas in search of migrating whales.

Some wear expressions of overwhelming bewilderment at all the boats and bustle.

THE WINGLIKE FLUKES OF A GRAY WHALE MAY MEASURE MORE THAN THREE METRES ACROSS. GRAY WHALES MAY GROW TO TWELVE OR THIRTEEN METRES LONG AND LIVE SIXTY OR EIGHTY YEARS. (STEVE SWARTZ PHOTO)

A common misconception among visitors from afar is that Vancouver Island is a salty backwater where stubble-faced, plaid-shirted lumberjacks are at perpetual loggerheads with mainland escapees and other social misfits. Few realize as they drive off the ferries that they've landed on the largest North American island in the Pacific, as big as the states of Maryland and Delaware combined, nine times the size of Long Island, New York. Nearly 600,000 people live here, and predictions are that at least another 240,000 will maroon themselves on this rock before the year 2016. Only two hundred kilometres down the island's coast from Tofino is the capital of Canada's third-largest province.

Each year the number of tourists that swarm the streets of Tofino is equivalent to the island's entire population. In two decades an isolated coastal settlement has become one of the nation's fastest-growing tourist meccas. It wasn't until 1958 that the village was linked to the outside world by gravel road. But it was a treacherous trek, a nerve-wracking 127-kilometre crawl over the Mackenzie Mountains, attempted mainly by the

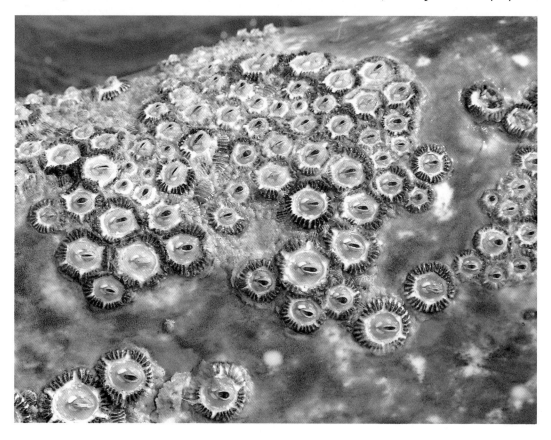

CRYPTOLEPAS RHACHIANECTI, A UNIQUE PARASITIC BARNACLE, INFESTS THE SKIN OF GRAY WHALES. NOT ALL WHALE SPECIES ARE PLAGUED BY BARNACLES, BUT THOSE THAT CARRY THEM EACH HAVE THEIR OWN PARTICULAR BRAND. WHILE THE BARNACLES MAY BE IRRITATING, THEY DON'T APPEAR TO POSE ANY SERIOUS HEALTH HAZARD. (STEVE SWARTZ PHOTO)

foolishly courageous and hopelessly curious. They risked life and limb, so it seemed, for the privilege of walking barefoot on the surf-battered shores of Long Beach.

But Long Beach was too good a secret to keep. By 1971, when Princess Anne came to British Columbia to officially open the park, that dirt track had become Highway 4, a freshly paved scenic route from the mill town of Port Alberni to the west coast—the only highway in B.C. that leads to the open Pacific. Within a decade, more than half a million visitors a year were coming to comb the beaches. By the early 1990s, after gray whales had become a prominent attraction, well over six hundred thousand a year were passing the portals of Pacific Rim National Park at Long Beach.

This new flood of tourists has taken Tofino by surprise. A once quaint and quiet fishing community has become a destination in its own right. It is suddenly saddled with maintaining its small-town aura in the face of inevitable change. New resorts, hotels, motels, lodges, bed-and-breakfast outlets, campgrounds, restaurants, tour boats, charter boats, and other tourist businesses are greeting the visitors. For the first time outside developers are looking at potential resort properties, land has become scarce, and values are moving beyond reach of many residents. With nowhere to park, fed up with summer lineups at the local grocery, frustrated Tofinoites wait anxiously for that first autumn downpour to swish the tourists from town, to bring just a few peaceful months before the return of the gray whales next spring.

The whales lure thousands of amateur naturalists to Long Beach. Wrapped in winter woollies and rain suits, they set up on rocky headlands to search for heart-shaped spouts beyond the surf line. For many, watching whales is a vacation theme, an excuse to explore Pacific Rim's thirty kilometres of dramatic coastal scenery; the never-ending sand beaches, virgin rain forests, eagles, seabirds, and sea lions. They're lulled to sleep by the soothing sound of breakers crashing on the shores and headlands. Many come to witness the fury of winter storms: they bundle up and step into the elements, stomping along the beaches, tasting the salt spray that spatters their faces, watching the giant cedars and sitka spruce sway in the furious gales.

The arrival of the gray whales in late February and early March kicks off the tourist season, and local entrepreneurs have no qualms about capitalizing on their whales. In Tofino there are the Whale Song Gallery, Orca Lodge, the Whale Centre. Forty kilometres to the south, on the opposite end of Long Beach, an Indian carving of a gray whale ushers visitors into Ucluelet, a village of fifteen hundred. Here are the Gray Whale Deli, Mo-B-Dick Video Rentals, the Whale's Tale Restaurant. The town's municipal stationery carries a logo of a gray whale with the slogan "Whale-Watching Capital of the World." It's a questionable claim: though as many as thirty thousand people a year may board whale-watching boats, and thousands more come to observe the migration from shore, the numbers hardly compare to the millions who sustain the California industry. By the early 1990s gray whale revenue at Pacific Rim was nonetheless significant: in an area populated by fewer than three thousand people, whale-watching fares alone were contributing nearly a million dollars a year to the local economy.

Since 1987 the migration has been celebrated with the Pacific Rim Whale Festival. While the whales swim past the park, on shore there are art shows, environmental plays, children's whale-colouring contests, family whale hunts, "spoutball" games, lectures, and films about whales and whaling.

On the beach outside the park's Wickaninnish Nature Centre, my family and others join park naturalist Steve Lobay. We follow him to the top of a grassy promontory, once used as an Indian defensive site. He sets up a spotting scope and hands out binoculars. "Scan the horizon for spouts," he says. Any we see will likely be on the move, plodding along at four or five kilometres an hour. "Once you've seen one with your naked eye, use your binoculars but look farther along to the north for it to resurface."

On still days the blast from a gray whale's blowholes can be heard a kilometre away as it shoots nearly five metres in the air. Though baleen whales have two blowholes, the spout appears as a single, vertical column, often divided at the top. If it is diving in deep water, say more than forty metres, it may blow five or six times, vanish for seven, eight, perhaps ten minutes, then resurface half a kilometre away. When it dives it rolls forward, exposing a series of bumps, or "knuckles," on the lower back where most other whales have dorsal fins. For shallow dives, a gray whale may take three or four breaths at intervals of ten or twenty seconds before diving for three or four minutes. It will reappear about three hundred metres away if it's travelling, but will stay in the area if feeding. When swimming in shallow water, gray whales appear pale, almost white on sunny days.

Before the end of an hour we've spotted seven whales, all within a kilometre of shore. Before the end of the day, what began as a pleasant pastime has become an addiction.

There's a low tide the next morning and we can walk to an island just off the beach and stay about four hours before an incoming tide will strand us. The clouds have cleared and steamy veils of vapour are rising from the sun-warmed sand. Near shore there's a greenish, tropical tinge to the sea. Beyond the island bright sunlight bounces off the frothy white surf.

"Did you see that?" my wife, Janet, shouts excitedly. "It jumped clear out of the water." We quicken our pace toward the island and settle on a rocky shelf facing the open sea. Below us two river otters munch a mussel, unperturbed by our intrusion.

"There! Right there!" Less than a kilometre out, the immense bulk of a breaching

gray whale comes splashing down in a frenzy of foam. The whale has hardly landed when another crashes through the surface. Two inflatable boats, their passengers clad in conspicuous orange survival suits, dash toward the whales. A pair of enormous flukes flashes in the sun and vanishes a hundred metres from the boats. Through binoculars we watch the boaters stop and wait. Suddenly a whale blows so close that everyone jumps to the opposite side of the boat, trying to escape the putrid stench of whale breath.

People who get close enough to look a gray whale in the eye see blotches of barnacles on the skin, particularly around the head. Like humpbacks, right whales, and some other species, gray whales carry their own brand of barnacles, as well as specific types of lice that scamper among the barnacles. Captain Charles Scammon earned the dubious distinction of having the gray whale's louse—*Cyamus scammoni*—named in his honour. Even at close range it's often difficult to discern the fuzz on the snout and the irregular rows of hairy bristles growing on top of the head and along the lower jaw.

Watching the whales breaching near the boats reminds me of a gray whale I'd seen farther down the coast from Long Beach. I was sitting on a rock when it burst through the surface and showered me with its fishy fragrance. It was the largest thing I'd seen come

GULLS AND FRIGATEBIRDS BEG FOR SHARK ENTRAILS DISCARDED BY MEXICAN FISHERMEN AT SAN IGNACIO LAGOON. RESEARCHERS HERE BEFRIENDED FISHERMEN, WHO OFTEN CATCH SHARKS IN THE FORTY- TO NINETY-KILOGRAM RANGE. THE UPTURNED TURTLE IN THE FOREGROUND HAS BEEN TAKEN ILLEGALLY. (DAVE MYERS PHOTO)

up from the sea—as long as a telephone pole but fat like a zeppelin. It puffed like a locomotive, then rolled headlong into the depths, its graceful tail blending with the emerald green of the ocean as it slipped away.

People were shouting. Behind me it seemed every camper on the beach was running to catch the whale. I was swept into the procession and we raced along the rocks, hopping over tide pools and gullies until we were blocked by an impassable surge channel. Suddenly the ocean opened and another cloud exploded over the animal's head. It moved out of reach and spent the rest of the afternoon lying listlessly in a kelp bed.

As hikers and beachcombers passed each other through the day whales were on their minds. Everyone had been captivated by this titanic creature from the deep. It was an event that drew total strangers to one another's campfires and filled us with optimism at the prospect of seeing it again.

The next morning we board a commercial whale-watching cruiser at Tofino. A foghorn sighs mournfully in the mist as the boat pitches and rolls through the Pacific swells. Yesterday's sun is gone: it's a dreary west-coast day—the drizzle settles around our collars and cuffs, and a twenty-knot southeaster bites unkindly at our faces. Yet for nearly an hour most of the forty passengers have stayed on deck, squinting toward a hazy horizon for plumes of vapour bursting from the blowholes of a whale. Who will spot the first whale?

"There's one!" comes a shout from the upper deck, and a voice through the P.A. system quickly announces: "Off the starboard bow, two o'clock." Instantly everyone is on their feet, rummaging through bags for binoculars and cameras. Pressed against the rails, scanning the waves fifty metres away, the wait is endless. One minute, three minutes, four...suddenly the great leviathan breaks the surface and a spout of steam fires four metres into the sky. Before a single shutter has clicked the whale is gone. But everyone has seen it now; everyone is anxious for another glimpse.

Before the whale resurfaces the mottled gray backs of two others appear simultaneously off the port side. Air and water shoot from their lungs, and momentary heart-shaped spouts are whisked away by the wind.

The skipper grins with satisfaction and launches into his practised spiel: less than two weeks ago these whales were swimming past Newport, Oregon, he says. They've now reached the halfway point on their journey to northern seas. The migration will peak here by Easter weekend, and before the end of May nearly all of the world's Pacific gray whales will have passed Vancouver Island.

* * *

Nearly all of the world's Pacific gray whales amounted to about eleven thousand animals in 1972 when Jim Darling began his research in these waters near Tofino. Now Canada's foremost authority on gray whales, Darling began his career as a surfer at Long Beach. While riding the waves in 1968, he noticed feeding whales enveloped by clouds of sand just beyond the surf line. Though intrigued, he gave it little thought at the time.

When the park, with its new flood of tourists, opened in the early 1970s he took a summer job skippering a boat that offered nature cruises. "The idea was to make money for school and do a bunch of surfing in between." The cruises concentrated on sea lions, seabirds, and other wildlife, but gray whales were often part of the scenery.

According to the science books, however, these whales weren't supposed to be here. A trip to the library revealed little about local gray whales: most of the literature focused on the southern one-third of the range and was largely based on casual observation and dead whales. One book said the empty stomachs of dissected whales proved that migrating grays rarely eat until they reach their northern feeding grounds. Another said they abruptly turn left at the forty-ninth parallel and head straight across the open ocean to the Bering and Chukchi seas.

Darling, of course, could see with his own eyes that none of this was true: he'd watched them feeding here in summer. Someone should study this, he thought, but after graduating in 1972 with a marine biology degree from the University of Victoria, life as an impoverished student didn't hold much appeal. Then the superintendent of Pacific Rim offered the princely sum of $4,000 for a literature review of gray whales in the park. Darling accepted the cash and bought a three-metre Zodiac which, when fully inflated, squeezed comfortably into the back of his van.

While completing his review, Darling met biologist Dave Hatler, who was doing a mammal survey for the park. Over dinner Darling mentioned he'd recently seen a gray whale with a conspicuous orange scar. Hatler immediately abandoned his meal, jumped up from the table, and returned with a box of photographs. He rummaged through them and produced a picture, taken in 1970, of a whale with an orange scar. "Is this the whale?"

A FRIENDLY GRAY WHALE SWIMS ALONGSIDE A WHALE-WATCHING BOAT NEAR TOFINO. AS MANY AS THIRTY THOUSAND PEOPLE A YEAR TAKE TO THE SEAS OFF SOUTHWEST VANCOUVER ISLAND IN SEARCH OF WILD WHALES. THE NORTHBOUND MIGRATION PAST THE ISLAND PEAKS IN LATE MARCH. ABOUT FORTY "RESIDENT" GRAYS SUSTAIN THE WHALE-WATCHING INDUSTRY THROUGH SUMMER. (JIM BORROWMAN PHOTO)

Determined to match the photograph, Darling scraped up enough to buy a camera and two-hundred-millimetre lens. Working as a park naturalist in 1973 and '74 he was often "required" to go out and watch whales. In his spare time he buzzed about in his Zodiac, photographing grays, collecting sighting reports from lightkeepers along the west coast of Vancouver Island. Eventually he managed to shoot the orange-scarred whale in both of those years, along with a few others that bore distinctive scars and scratches which, with variations in skin pigmentation, allowed him to identify specific animals. Hatler and Darling wrote a paper in 1974 describing their repeated sightings of "Orange Scar" and "Whitepatch," a whale with an obvious white patch just below the dorsal hump, photographed near Long Beach at Wickaninnish Bay in 1972 and '73.

They had disproved the notion that whale facts can be gleaned only from dead animals. In a 1971 paper entitled *The Life History and Ecology of the Gray Whale*, D. W. Rice and A. A. Wolman, who had examined the carcasses of many grays killed for research, said: "Individual whales cannot be observed repeatedly, therefore knowledge of most aspects of their life history must be deduced from data provided by examining a large series of specimens." By the time the paper was published, Dr. Roger Payne, of the New York Zoological Society, had already begun studying wild right whales in Argentina through photo-identification.

Mike Bigg, then the only marine mammalogist on Canada's west coast, encouraged Darling to perfect his photo-identification process. The most practical way to pursue field studies was to begin a master's program and become affiliated with a university. "I wasn't crazy about school," says Darling. "I wasn't dying to go back." He approached Dr. Dean Fisher at UBC but failed to get an enthusiastic hearing.

"We laugh about it now," says Darling, "but at that time nobody was studying living whales. Mike was just starting with killer whales. Roger Payne was just a couple of years ahead. It was a really new thing. It was developing in different parts of the world, but totally separate, totally unplanned." He proposed his studies to Dr. John McInerney, of the University of Victoria, who gave him a credit card for boat gas, just in time to catch the 1975 migration.

"At that point no one had seen the migration up here. Gordon Pike, a Department of Fisheries biologist, had written about it from lighthouse reports in the sixties, but no one had looked at this migration. We weren't even sure if it was for real. Do the whales just sort of pass by unknown to anybody or is it visible, is it something you can actually see?"

The operators of a Tofino airline raised their eyebrows suspiciously when Darling

A NEWBORN GRAY WHALE SUR-FACES IN THE MURKY WATERS OF SAN IGNACIO LAGOON, ONE OF THREE MEXICAN SANCTU-ARIES FOR BREEDING GRAY WHALES. DURING THE MATING SEASON, FROM LATE DECEMBER TO MID-APRIL, SAN IGNACIO MAY BE INHABITED BY SIX HUNDRED OR MORE GRAY WHALES. MOST COWS BEAR ONE CALF EVERY TWO YEARS, WHILE A FEW PRODUCE AN OFFSPRING NEAR-LY EVERY YEAR. (STEVE SWARTZ PHOTO)

AS A SUMMER SURFER IN 1969, JIM DARLING NOTICED FEEDING GRAY WHALES ENVELOPED IN CLOUDS OF SILT NEAR LONG BEACH, ON VANCOUVER ISLAND. HE LATER DOCUMENTED THE ANNUAL MIGRATION OF GRAY WHALES PAST THE ISLAND, AND DISCOVERED THAT A GROUP OF "RESIDENT" GRAYS FEEDS IN THE AREA THROUGH SUMMER. DR. DARLING IS NOW CONSIDERED CANADA'S FOREMOST AUTHORITY ON PACIFIC GRAY WHALES. (BRUCE OBEE PHOTO)

asked a pilot to take him out to find the gray-whale migration.

"Where is it?" the pilot inquired.

"I don't know," Darling replied, "but they're supposed to be heading up the island at this time. I have lighthouse reports that say they go by."

"How far out?"

"I don't know. It's supposed to be along the coast. I doubt if it's out more than a few miles."

So they climbed aboard a floatplane and headed over the open sea toward Japan. As the mountains of Vancouver Island shrank behind them the pilot announced they were running out of fuel: they'd have to return. Not a single whale was spotted. "They thought I was nuts," Darling recalls with some embarrassment.

Only a few days later, he and a friend took a boat off Long Beach and ran across dozens of whales. They returned day after day to photograph Pacific grays parading past the park. "I found that in fact there was this incredible thing happening on the coast which, at that point, essentially was not publicly known."

His research was given a boost in 1975 when McInerney sent him to Bloomington, Indiana, for a whale conference. The key speaker was Roger Payne, who was gaining a reputation as one of the world's most outstanding cetologists. He showed a film that was "just a knockout," depicting photo-identification techniques similar to those being developed by Darling. Payne, however, had gotten an earlier start: Darling could learn from his mistakes. Payne agreed to join Mike Bigg as one of Darling's supervisors for his master's work.

Once it was established that these animals do, in fact, migrate within view of Vancouver Island, Darling found that the first northbound whales appear in late February. After peaking in the last two weeks of March, the numbers decline, with a few stragglers moving through in late May and early June. Southbound migrants arrive at Long Beach in November; they are most plentiful in the latter half of December, and from mid-January to February, sightings are rare. Few whales are spotted on the southbound migration because of winter gales.

Many, if not most whales are seen within two kilometres of shore, some as close as thirty metres. Researchers in the 1960s speculated that gray whales orient themselves by locating coastal landmarks, both below and above the water, and by following depth contours. Darling has often seen gray whales breach before deciding on which side to pass a reef. He has also watched them retrace a route, then move into deeper water to navigate a channel.

"The animals closely follow the coastline, some farther offshore in straight unbroken headings, some inshore almost rebounding off rocks and underwater shoals," he says. "It seems reasonable that whales would use sight, sound, and depth clues to follow the coast and some may be more experienced than others. Certainly the crossing of wide channels, the entrances to sounds, or straits creates some confusion for at least some of the whales."

Travelling whales seem unaffected by inclement weather, but for scientists with cameras, weather off Vancouver Island's west coast isn't always cooperative. The shores, exposed to the full force of North Pacific swells, are continually buffeted by prevailing westerlies and southeast winds that frequently blow fifteen to thirty knots in the whale-watching season. And anyone who has been to Long Beach knows "west is wet": Tofino is drenched annually by an average annual rainfall of 3230 millimetres—ten and a half feet. A big blow may last two to four days, but a series of storms can landlock boaters for weeks. When the weather stabilizes, particularly in late summer and early fall, heavy fog often consumes the coast or settles just offshore, waiting to be dissipated by fresh rain. "Even during summer the weather and ocean conditions permitted observation from boats on only about 50 percent of available days," Darling writes in his master's thesis.

On clear days whales were located and photographed from small boats. Feeding whales could easily be pinpointed during weekly flights by the silty sand-trails they churned up from the bottom. Both sides of each whale were shot from within a hundred metres and skin patterns were sketched on a data chart. When the field work was completed in 1976, Darling faced the monumental task of sorting through forty-five hundred photographs.

Matching these pictures, taken over four field seasons, confirmed that not all whales at Long Beach are passing through. Each year between thirty-five and fifty "residents," as Darling calls them, drop out of the northbound migration, forage off the island's west coast through summer, then join the southbound migration in autumn. They arrive at the peak of the migration and usually leave around October; the latest a summer resident has been identified at Long Beach is December 14. Today these lingering gray whales help sustain whale-watching businesses through summer, after the spring migrants have passed.

Since completing his master's work, Darling has continued to monitor migrating and resident whales off Vancouver Island. Some whales come back every year; others return sporadically. Over six summers from 1975 to 1981, ninety-three whales were identified. Of those whales, fifty-six appeared in only one season, while thirty-seven were seen in more than one year. By 1984 one resident whale had been spotted during eight seasons and a number of others had been seen for seven summers.

The shallow, sandy-bottomed seafloor off Long Beach resembles the feeding grounds of the Bering and Chukchi seas. Many of the resident whales return to exactly the same places at the same time each summer. Others feed at several sites, with no particular schedule. Some may travel nearly eighty kilometres from one feeding site to another; others may choose four destinations, covering forty kilometres in one week. A few are known to forage in Wickaninnish Bay for more than eighty days in a single season.

Contrary to early assumptions that migrating gray whales save their appetites for northern waters, Darling believes that southwest Vancouver Island is one of several pockets of feeding areas along the migration route. About seventy-five grays summer off the Oregon coast and a few residents inhabit western Washington waters. The number of resident whales along these coasts hasn't grown with the general population: perhaps they are all the habitat can support.

Early in his research, Darling thought he had dispelled another myth when he spent nearly two hours witnessing what appeared to be a trio of mating whales. They were rising out of the water, throat to throat, belly to belly, vigorously shaking flukes and pectoral fins. His master's thesis describes the scene. "Several times a whale would roll, belly up, and a large flesh-coloured penis 1-1.5 m. in length, perhaps 25-35 cm. across the base and narrowing to a slim point, erected in an arch, would show. At one point two whales rolled simultaneously, both showing penes. These two lay side by side, belly up, with one's penis on the other's underside. Then they intertwined penes for several minutes. Following several more minutes of similar activity all three whales rolled belly up simultaneously and all with semi-erect penes. All three were males."

Homosexuality among males, particularly juveniles, may be common, but it's unlikely that any true mating occurs outside their southern calving areas. It was also thought that "friendlies" were found only in the south, but in 1983 the first friendly whale showed up near Long Beach. Darling and an assistant were photo-identifying six or seven whales near Meares Island, off Tofino, travelling from whale to whale in a skiff. One whale came toward the boat and surfaced, tail first. Next thing they knew it was directly under the boat.

"If I hadn't been through it all in Mexico, and was aware of it, I probably would have moved away." In one of several incidents involving friendlies at San Ignacio Lagoon, a whale approached Darling's boat from behind, closed its mouth around the propeller, and pulled the boat backwards.

They spent hours with the friendly at Meares Island while it rubbed the boat, banged the hull, and pushed them around with its rostrum. Darling and his friend agreed to keep this whale secret, fearing the widespread attention—and possible harassment—that would come with word of its whereabouts. They managed to keep it quiet for about a month, until someone saw them interacting with the whale. A picture appeared on the front page of the *Vancouver Sun* and the whale's solitude was shattered by throngs of boaters.

"It turned into an absolute circus," Darling says angrily. "I was embarrassed by the reaction of the local people." He wrote articles warning people that this was a wild creature, not to be disturbed, begging them to enjoy it but give it space. "People were out there tearing off their clothes and leaping off the bows of their boats onto the back of this animal. There were dogs jumping from the front of the boats onto the whale's back. Local people were running the thing over: it was absolutely atrocious."

One would hope that with today's more enlightened environmental attitudes that mistreatment of whales is a thing of the past. Yet despite the accumulation of knowledge, people still tend to view whales in a different light from other wildlife, to anthropomorphize about their needs and habits.

"The intrigue is sort of with the mysticism, almost more than with the animal. I think people don't treat them as wild animals," says Darling. "There's this image of the whale as something that is not the same as a wild bear, or any other wild animal. Consequently I think whales have proven to be incredibly tolerant of people and, in fact, have managed to include boats and other things within their daily behaviour pattern, like when gray whales rub on boats, or when killer whales and dolphins bow ride. There are a lot of situations when the whales actually interact with boats.

"I guess that's led to the feeling that these things are something different than other wild animals. But I don't think they are, and I think there will be cases where it would be better if people were perhaps just a little bit wary of the animals. Accidents will come eventually just because of the volume of people who come close to the whales."

Since whale-watching came to Long Beach in the early 1980s, the question of whether it is harmful arises periodically. "In the summer here it has built up to the point where there can be one little whale that's in, say, Ahous Bay on Vargas Island, and there'll be three or four or five whale-watching boats and a couple of airplanes looking at it all day long, every day, not to mention kayakers and private boats. Add them all up and it can be constant.

"We know that mammals react to stress, to disturbances, and we know that different species react in different ways. Some are very adaptable, some aren't, but stress over a long period can affect our health."

Commercial whale-watchers are careful not to bother the animals, and Darling believes that, at least for the moment, the benefits of taking people to see whales outweigh any disturbance. But the industry is large enough that Canada should replace its informal whale-watching guidelines with protective legislation like that of the United States. Laws regulating the number of boats, distances from whales, the sharing by commercial operators of areas near whales, and methods of approaching the animals are needed.

"All in all, I think it's terrific. It's great that people are getting out and seeing whales in the wild. It's really nice to see that people are so interested."

* * *

If whale-watching is an issue at all, it's an easy one for the public to understand. To look beyond that simplicity to broader habitat concerns requires more commitment than most people are willing to make. Yet the larger picture is really the issue when mapping the future for our wildlife.

"I think we've convinced most of the world, certainly the western world, that whales should be saved," says Darling. "I think 90 percent of anybody you talk to would agree with that. But probably 5 percent of the people realize that means you have to save their food supply too. Probably only 1 percent understand that saving the food supply means maintaining the integrity of the system which supports the food. Very few people realize that this is all tied together with development. I don't think it's very deep, the understanding, yet the public certainly decides the fate of the animals: there's no question about that."

THE GRAY WHALE— *ESCHRICHTIUS ROBUSTUS*—IS THE ONLY MEMBER OF THE ESCHRICHTIIDAE FAMILY. KNOWN FOR ITS ROBUST BODY AND KNUCKLELIKE DORSAL FIN, ITS MOTTLED GREY COLOURING IS UNLIKE ANY OTHER WHALE. IT ALSO HAS A GREATER VARIETY OF FEEDING METHODS THAN OTHER CETACEANS. (STEVE SWARTZ PHOTO)

In Ahous Bay, eight kilometres west of Tofino, Darling and I scan the ocean for the spouts of surfacing whales. The beaches here are like the sandy shores of Long Beach, prime feeding territory for gray whales. There are no whales here today: they're likely farther south, says Darling, where I'd seen them from the deck of a whale-watching boat earlier in the migration.

On the bottom below us, however, there is probably oil from the *Nestucca* spill. On December 22, 1988, the *Nestucca*, an oil barge, collided with the tug that was towing it off Grays Harbor, Washington, nearly three hundred kilometres south of Long Beach. Some 875,000 litres of Bunker C oil—a syrupy, black tar—poured through the holed hull and spread along the beaches from central Washington to northern Vancouver Island. The Canadian Department of Fisheries and Oceans contracted Darling to conduct a survey of gray-whale feeding areas after the spill. Fourteen sediment samples from five sites contained hydrocarbons, oil, and grease. "Those were just random samples. And we found traces of oil in every one."

Although the gray whale feeds by various methods, its most common technique is to scrape along sandy seafloors, sucking in silt and sand laden with bottom-dwelling crustaceans, such as amphipods, and other invertebrates. With the force of a fourteen-hundred-kilogram tongue, it expels the sand through baleen plates, trapping its food in a web of bristles. While divers in the survey sites didn't find oil, they did locate trenches scoured by recently-feeding whales. On shore, oil still soiled the beaches more than two years later.

There are too many unanswered questions to judge the effects of the oil on gray whales. What hydrocarbon levels naturally occur in these sediments? How do they influence the feed? How much oil can a whale tolerate in its food? How flexible is a gray whale in switching to other foods?

"Whales are built to eat," says Darling. "When you look at trying to understand the animal the first thing you do is look at its food supply. It really governs their entire behaviour throughout the whole year, including their mating behaviour."

As executive director of the West Coast Whale Research Foundation, with a field station near his home in Tofino, Darling continues to work with gray whales. He has focused lately on feeding habits and the effects of human activities on food sources. Little is known of the impact of oil spills, herring-roe fishing, or geoduck harvesting. By analyzing bottom sediments, plankton from the water column, and scat samples, Darling hopes to determine when, where, and why they feed on different types of marine life.

"We realize that these whales could go away tomorrow. We could make some guesses as to why they weren't here, but we really wouldn't know."

* * *

Beyond Vancouver Island, migrating gray whales swim past both sides of the Queen Charlotte Islands and hug the shoreline across the Gulf of Alaska. They funnel through Unimak Pass, near the western end of the Alaska Peninsula, then spread over the Bering and Chukchi seas. For nearly half the year, from June to October, they forage in the fertile feeding waters over the continental shelf, usually at depths of less than seventy metres, until the seas begin to freeze. Those off Barrow, Alaska, on the Arctic Ocean, start moving south in August. By late October the first southbound migrants leave the Bering Sea through Unimak Pass, where the migration peaks in early December.

In 1988 three Pacific grays lingered too long near Barrow and were imprisoned by advancing pack ice. An entire community of Inuit attempted to rescue the whales, cutting breathing holes in the ice with axes and chainsaws. Then a helicopter, dangling a giant concrete torpedo, punched a line of holes toward the sea. But the whales, able to breathe in open water near shore, refused to follow the holes, which quickly froze. A bulldozer, attempting to break through a wall of ice at the mouth of the bay, bogged down in the frozen snow shortly before the youngest whale died. Finally, as television viewers around the world watched anxiously, the Russian icebreaker *Admiral Makarov* rammed through the ice wall and bashed a path to the waiting whales. After three weeks of confinement they swam to freedom, while Russians, Americans, and Inuit celebrated on shore.

In these northern seas gray whales feed mainly on the bottom, but this species has a greater range of feeding methods than any of the great whales. It takes pelagic prey by skimming along the surface with its mouth open; it herds spawning squid or baitfish into a circle and devours them. Like the humpback, the gray whale may swim up from below its prey with its enormous mouth agape. It swims through kelp beds, gobbling herring roe and mycids. Sometimes it simply treads water against a tide, letting plankton flow across its baleen plates. Mary Lou Jones watched one swimming along the surface, slurping down paddies of floating eel grass. Having a number of feeding methods reduces the gray whale's dependence on a single prey, probably giving it greater dietary flexibility.

"Perhaps it is for this reason that the Pacific gray whale population has persisted through geologic time, has recovered from severe exploitation, and remains today one of the least endangered of the great whales," writes Mary Nerini, in a paper entitled *A Review of Gray Whale Feeding Ecology*.

INUIT FROM BARROW, ALASKA, ATTEMPT TO RESCUE ENTRAPPED GRAY WHALES BY CUTTING THROUGH THE ICE WITH CHAIN SAWS. THREE WHALES LINGERED TOO LONG IN THEIR SUMMER FEEDING WATERS BEFORE RETURNING TO THEIR SOUTHERN WINTERING GROUNDS. ONE WHALE DIED, BUT TWO WERE RESCUED WHEN A RUSSIAN ICEBREAKER BASHED A PATH TO THE OPEN SEA. (MARK FRAKER PHOTOS)

In 1980, Nerini used side-scan sonar to survey a large section of seafloor in the Chirikov Basin of the Bering Sea. The sonar provided images portraying the sizes and shapes of feeding depressions made by gray whales.

Nerini estimates that the oil content in the blubber of a gray whale feeding here increases by an average of 5,063 kilograms—about 16 to 30 percent of its total body weight. Conservatively, she says, one whale would ingest 61,370 kilograms of prey in five months. A single whale would remove amphipods from twenty-three hectares of bottom sediment. If 15,550 gray whales were feeding here, each year they would turn over 3,565 square kilometres of ocean floor, or about 9 percent of the amphipod community.

"The gray whale may be unusual among whales in that, in addition to being an important predator, it is also a major source of physical disturbance to the exploited

community. In concert with currents, sea ice, and storm waves, the gray whale may be responsible for clearing space which can be later colonized by the prime prey species. In this way, it may help to maintain the very amphipod community it exploits."

Certainly the gray whale's feeding habits and its propensity for shallow waters have contributed to its remarkable recovery. "Gray whales hang along the coast and, let's face it, continental shelves are productive, especially along the eastern coast of the Pacific," says Steve Swartz. "The upwelling phenomenon, the whole production-driving machine there. Wherever they go there's always something to eat and generally lots of it. So they've had a reliable source of food for a long time. That, with their general biology and tenacious attitude, has contributed to them coming up in numbers when some of these other populations haven't."

"It'll remain to be seen just what the population does. We're going to have to, as a scientific endeavour, continue to watch them, to carefully monitor that population. That's going to take a commitment. Then as managers, what we glean from that, how successful those efforts have been, might just help us with things like right whales, humpbacks, and populations that aren't coming back as readily."

Because they're not hunted or endangered, governments are reluctant to fund the study of gray whales. "But there could be major justification to carry on gray whale studies," says Jim Darling. "They're probably tremendous indicators of the surrounding system."

WATER STREAMS FROM THE FLUKES OF A DIVING GRAY WHALE IN MEXICAN WATERS. EARLY WHALERS REDUCED THIS SPECIES TO NEAR EXTINCTION BEFORE IT WAS PROTECTED IN 1946. NOW, WITH MORE THAN TWENTY-ONE THOUSAND ROAMING THE NORTH PACIFIC, IT MAY BECOME THE FIRST CETACEAN TO BE REMOVED FROM THE U.S. ENDANGERED SPECIES LIST. (DAVE MYERS PHOTO)

Humpbacks, Minkes and Miscellany

"Humpbacks, dead ahead!" Jim Borrowman calls from the wheelhouse of the *Lukwa*. "Five of them." Everyone scrambles up the companionway to scope the waters of Fitz Hugh Sound, eager to substantiate the helmsman's claim.

"There," Graeme Ellis says calmly, "three blows."

"I say five," Borrowman argues. He puts down his binoculars and eases the throttle ahead. Again the whales blow; again I miss them. While the others debate numbers I squint into the distance and see only choppy seas. The skipper pushes the throttle up another notch and heads the boat toward Calvert Island. Near the entrance to Safety Cove two whales surface together, followed by another off our port bow.

"My God," I gasp to myself. These creatures are immense, the size of a city bus. I can count to ten in the time it takes one to lift its monstrous form into view, blow, and roll back into the murky depths. Suddenly a pair of serrated flukes, like giant outstretched eagle wings, heave from the surface in a cascade of water and follow the whale out of our world into its own.

"Told you we'd find 'em here," Borrowman grins. He'd invited me aboard with a promise of locating humpbacks off the eastern side of Calvert Island, where Fitz Hugh Sound and Rivers Inlet meet, 130 kilometres north of the *Lukwa's* home port at Telegraph Cove.

WITH ITS PECTORAL FINS OUT-STRETCHED, A FULL-GROWN HUMPBACK WHALE BREACHES IN WATERS NEAR LAHAINA, ON THE ISLAND OF MAUI. THESE GREAT LEVIATHANS, THE MOST ACRO-BATIC OF THE GREAT WHALES, ENTERTAIN THOUSANDS OF HAWAIIAN WHALE-WATCHERS.

At the end of the whale-watching season Borrowman and his partner, Bill Mackay, often take a few friends for a cruise up the central B.C. coast to look for cetaceans and miscellaneous marine mammals.

These humpbacks may have spent the summer in the Gulf of Alaska or Bering Sea and are making their way to winter mating waters off Hawaii or Mexico. Or they could be among a few which remain in these northerly climes through the year, feeding near the mouths of mainland fjords, occasionally taking short forays into Puget Sound or Georgia Strait.

Humpbacks feed by various methods, sifting krill, anchovies, herring, or other small fish through baleen plates that hang seventy-five centimetres from their upper jaws. Their pleated throat grooves expand like an accordion as they strain water through their baleen. Sometimes they lie lazily on their sides, sucking in prey on the surface. A more aggressive hunting method is known as "lunge feeding": they plough through the water with their mouths agape, scooping food as they swim. Their most intriguing technique is "bubble-net feeding." Below the surface, one or two whales swim in circles around a school of fish, blowing bubbles as they move. As a mass of bubbles rises, the frightened fish gather in a tight ball in the centre of the "net" and the whales swim up from below with their mouths wide open.

"Better get the speedboat ready," Craig Matkin suggests. We haul in the tow line while Matkin and Ellis don cruiser suits and check their camera gear. Matkin's wife, Olga von Ziegesar, has been studying humpbacks in Alaska's Prince William Sound since 1980. He'd vowed to photo-identify any he encountered while cruising these B.C. waters to see if they match pictures of Alaskan whales.

Humpbacks are known for their fluke flashing, and individuals are identified through pictures of the undersides of their tails. Often more than five metres across, fluke shapes vary noticeably. Some are slender and pointed; others are wide, like the wings of a sharp-shinned hawk or the petals of a sunflower. They may be entirely black, white, or a mottled mix of both, and they carry distinctive scars, even major wounds from orca or shark attacks. Some flukes are smooth along the outer edges; others resemble the teeth of a dull saw.

From the foredeck of the *Lukwa* I share the frustration of scientists trying to identify whales. While they're photographing the animals, I'm flustered in my efforts to get whales and researchers in the same picture. It's a squally day: one moment the sun reflects from the backs of the whales; the next minute clouds and drizzle darken the sky—barely enough light for their three-hundred-millimetre lenses. The whales must be feeding: there's no direction to their movements. They dive and the skiff heads on the course they were taking; after an endless wait two whales surface a hundred metres astern of the boat. The skiff whips around to catch their fleeting flukes and the third animal blows right where the boat has just been.

BUBBLE STREAMING, LIKE SING-
ING, MAY BE A SIGN OF AGGRES-
SION, OFTEN SEEN WHEN MALES
VIE FOR THE RIGHT TO ESCORT
A COW AND CALF. THIS WHALE
IS CHASING A GROUP OF FALSE
KILLER WHALES THAT WERE
FEEDING ON A MAHI-MAHI, OR
DOLPHIN FISH. SIMILAR EXHALA-
TIONS OCCUR WHEN HUMPBACKS
FEED BY "BUBBLE-NETTING."

Timing is crucial. From the first blow there's a minute, maybe two, to position the boat behind the whale while it blows three or four times more, then hoists its heavy tail clear of the water and flips it ventral-side-up for the photographers. Motor-driven cameras snap half a dozen shots as the whale slips away to stay down ten or fifteen minutes. Patience, precision, practice, persistence. Always guessing where the subject will next appear. The art of whale photography is a lifelong mission.

After more than an hour they've successfully photo-identified two whales but the third refuses to fluke. Time after time they race into position behind the beast: it makes a final blow then lifts its tail almost—but not quite—out of the water. Through binoculars I'm sure I hear Matkin mumbling his quiet curses. This whale is not a fluker: the skiff returns to the *Lukwa*. Matkin seems mildly disappointed, but concedes that two out of three is not bad. We assure him that the entire ordeal is video-taped, evidence for his wife of his valiant effort.

The photographs taken by von Ziegesar and Matkin are among thousands which have helped identify individual humpback whales throughout the North Pacific. Humpbacks are found in all oceans of the world and the fine-tuning of research methods for the species, such as photo-identification, has been done in both the Atlantic and Pacific. Pictures not only help scientists understand migrations and behaviour, but provide some basis for population estimates, although they still vary widely.

In the North Pacific before 1905, there were probably 15,000 humpbacks. But humpbacks, like gray whales, suffered serious losses to whalers and, to a lesser degree, aboriginal hunters: over the next two decades more than 13,000 were killed in Hawaiian and Mexican waters, nearly 3,400 were taken off Oregon and Washington, over 2,800 were caught off B.C., and almost 4,000 were harpooned in Alaska. By 1966, when hunting humpbacks was banned worldwide, there may have been only 1,000 left in the North Pacific. By the early 1980s, 1,056 individuals had been identified in Hawaii, 420 in southeast Alaska, 54 in Prince William Sound, 8 in B.C., and 12 in Mexico's Revillagigedo Islands. Today about 3,500 have been photo-identified in the North Pacific, including more than 200 in Japan, and total population estimates vary between 5,000 and 10,000.

Dissuaded by storm warnings to venture off the outside of Calvert Island, we continue up Fitz Hugh Sound, past Hakai Passage, to the old cannery town of Namu. A few halibut boats, their big orange buoys bulging off the aft decks, are tied to the dock. An aging fisherman, in gumboots, tattered gray jersey, and woollen pants with suspenders, is chatting with fisheries officers aboard the *Robson Reef*.

Above the docks the boardwalks and buildings are surprisingly shipshape, considering they've seen little use in recent years. This town is not quite dead: the minimarket, post office, liquor store, and administration buildings are still operating; a caretaker walks about with a jangle of keys hanging from his belt. The cafe, schoolhouse, green and white cottages, the bunkhouses—formerly the "Namu Hilton"—are shut tight. B.C. Packers, which once owned more than thirty canneries, is in the midst of finalizing the sale of Namu to entrepreneurs with sport-fishing and tourism dreams.

It was near Namu, in 1965, that two fishermen caught the first killer whale to take up residence in a public aquarium. To many, Namu is the name of a whale, not a coastal

MORE THAN THREE THOUSAND NORTH PACIFIC HUMPBACK WHALES HAVE BEEN IDENTIFIED THROUGH PHOTOGRAPHS OF THE UNDERSIDES OF THEIR FLUKES. THESE TAILS, OFTEN MORE THAN FIVE METRES ACROSS, VARY NOTICEABLY IN SHAPE AND COLOUR.

community. Yet in its heyday, Namu was a seasonal home for six hundred cannery workers. Founded in 1893, it has survived a major fire, a complete reconstruction, and a coast-wide fishermen's strike. By the mid-1970s the plant was no longer operating at full capacity. By the early '90s, with modernization and a declining fishery, Namu was obsolete—another subtle signal that the resource industries of the twentieth century won't keep us afloat in the twenty-first.

The morning mist has lifted above the Coast Mountains and we head down the inside edge of Calvert Island toward the open waters of Queen Charlotte Sound. Beyond the entrance to Rivers Inlet a gentle swell rolls in from the west. In the distance I discern peculiar splashes, like whitecaps, stretched in a long line. They're moving our way.

"What's that?" I ask. Ellis looks through the wheelhouse windows with binoculars. "Lags," he smiles, knowing we're in for some fun. "Pacific white-sided dolphins. Let's speed it up a bit, Bill."

Mackay pushes the throttle ahead to eighteen hundred rpm and the boat picks up to seventeen knots, throwing out a foaming white wake, raising the roar of the engines. Camcorders and cameras are yanked from cases and we spread around the boat to greet the onslaught. A hundred, perhaps more, are porpoising straight for us from both sides. It's an ambush: in moments we're surrounded. They're zooming through the bow wake, splashing off the port and starboard sides, bucking the waves off the stern. My camera almost falls in the sea as I lie on my stomach and hang out over the bow, shooting down at dolphins swimming centimetres below the speeding boat.

For close to an hour they entertain us, leaping through the waves as we zigzag a course to nowhere, whizzing around in circles and figure-eights. Then, as suddenly as they came, they're gone, like shorebirds flushed by a raptor. Mackay eases back on the throttle and puts the boat in neutral. We're adrift on an empty sea: I feel my heart pumping adrenalin through my veins. Then everyone starts to laugh. Mackay puts the boat in gear and heads toward the Sea Otter Group, a cluster of barren islets off the south end of Calvert Island.

About halfway out, Matkin, Ellis, and I board the skiff and slice through the swells to Pearl Rocks. These islets, along with nearby Virgin Rocks, are a year-round haulout for Steller's sea lions. Together they were once one of several breeding rookeries along this coast but, like most other sea-lion sites, it was devastated by a "control program." To appease fishermen complaining of unfair competition, fisheries officers machine-gunned a total of 29,800 sea lions in the Sea Otter Group between 1913 and 1939. Seventy-one hundred were pups. Not surprisingly, the animals abandoned the rookery, but later established these rocks as a haulout. More than a thousand have been counted here since the carnage ended.

PACIFIC WHITE-SIDED DOLPHINS, OFTEN TRAVELLING IN SCHOOLS OF A HUNDRED OR MORE, LOVE TO RIDE IN THE BOW AND STERN WAKES OF FAST-RUNNING BOATS. DOZENS MAY CONVERGE ON A VESSEL, LEAPING AND SWIMMING JUST BELOW THE SURFACE WITHIN A METRE OF THE BOAT, FOLLOWING IT FOR AN HOUR OR MORE BEFORE SUDDENLY VANISHING.

The "control program" continued at other sites until 1968. Today some six thousand Steller's sea lions in B.C. produce about twelve hundred pups a year, breeding in three rookeries along this coast. The closest is the Scott Islands, eighty kilometres southwest of the Sea Otter Group. Another is at Cape St. James, the southern tip of the Queen Charlotte Islands. The most northerly is in Hecate Strait at North Danger Rocks. Just twenty kilometres north of the B.C. border, Alaska's Forrester Island produces about twenty-three hundred pups a year. After each breeding season, bulls and juveniles disperse from the breeding rocks to winter haulouts, leaving cows to contend with newborns near the breeding rookeries. About 70 percent of B.C.'s sea lions return to the rookeries to produce offspring. The other 30 percent occupy year-round haulouts like these at Pearl and Virgin rocks.

Ellis, one eye on the water, the other on the chart, keeps a distance as we explore the haulouts. Reefs protrude ominously through the surface each time a swell passes over.

SMALL FISH POUR FROM THE MOUTH OF A LUNGE-FEEDING MINKE WHALE AS IT SHOOTS THROUGH THE SURFACE, EXHALING STEAMY MIST THROUGH ITS BLOWHOLES. WITH ITS THROAT PLEATS EXTENDED, THE WHALE SWALLOWS ITS TINY PREY IN GREAT GULPS. AN UNDERWATER PHOTOGRAPHER ONCE WATCHED A HERRING SCHOOL PROGRESSIVELY SHRINK AS A MINKE REPEATEDLY PASSED THROUGH IT.

The sea lions are noticeably bothered by our presence, uneasily propped up on their foreflippers, growling anxiously as we putter along the outside edge of the reefs. A few drag their blubbery bodies to low-lying ledges and dive into the sea. Some of these big bulls weigh a tonne and measure three metres long.

"That looks like a seal," I say, pointing halfway up the islet. Ellis glances over the rocks then peers through a telephoto lens.

"It's a sea lion pup," he says, somewhat surprised. "This season's."

"It's too little to have swum here," I suggest.

"You're right," he replies. "It had to be born here, recently. Maybe they've begun breeding here again. Get a shot of that." This is encouraging: no breeding rookeries have been re-established for decades.

Careful to avoid rocks, Ellis pilots the boats through the swells toward kelp beds off the north end of the islet. This is prime sea-otter habitat—open sea, acres of kelp, treacherous reefs. Each time my binoculars rest on a bulbous kelp float I think I see the fuzzy face of a sea otter. We could look all day here, probably even see an otter, but fail to distinguish it from the kelp.

We give up the search and mosey up the outer shore of Calvert Island. Just south of Herbert Point a man dressed in dark brown is leaning against a rock above the water. Here, on the Pacific edge of the continent. As we approach, it's no longer a man, but a large otter; closer still, it's a black bear. Then, awakened by our outboard, a big head swings around and staring out from below the pronounced forehead are the eyes of a California sea lion.

Another revelation. Until now the northern extremity of the California sea lion's range was thought to be Solander Island, off the west coast of Vancouver Island, 150 kilometres due south of here. About four thousand Californias swim from their southern breeding waters each year to share winter haulouts in B.C. with the native Steller's sea lions. This lone animal indicates they may be extending their range, and perhaps increasing their numbers in these waters.

Outside the entrance to Hakai Pass, at the top end of Calvert Island, we pull astern of the *Lukwa* and tie the skiff. "You missed the minke," says Borrowman.

"What minke?"

"We thought it was a humpback. It was just floating around, not doing much."

I'm sorry I missed it: we don't see minkes that often, though a few inhabit these waters. Only about ten metres long, the minke is one of the smallest baleen whales, yet it is among the cetaceans known as finners, which include the twenty-six-metre, hundred-tonne blue whale, the largest animal on earth. The minke is probably the most acrobatic of finners, often breaching when feeding, jumping right out of the water, turning and coming down on its back.

Minkes feed mainly on zooplankton and small schooling fish like herring or sand lance. They often shoot through the surface into flocks of frantically feeding gulls, with tiny silver fish falling from their gigantic mouths. Once in a while they inadvertently swallow a bird. Underwater photographer Flip Nicklin once watched a school of herring progressively shrink as a minke whale repeatedly passed through the school. In Johnstone Strait, feeding minke whales have been known to pay no attention to killer whales— residents and mammal-eating transients—passing nearby.

Through the 1980s, researchers in B.C., Washington, and California photo-identified minkes. With pictures of dorsal fins, skin pigmentation, and small oval scars common to the species, they catalogued thirty in the San Juan Islands and seventeen in Monterey Bay. Another eight were identified in Johnstone Strait, mainly by people studying orcas. Some were seen year after year, frequently in the same places. They appear to have specific feeding sites. Minkes in the San Juans, for example, are most reliably seen in four separate areas between June and September.

No cow-calf pairs have been observed in these northern areas, suggesting the lactation period is so short that calves are weaned before they reach their summer feeding waters. Little is known of their winter distribution and no calving grounds have been found.

We drop anchor for the night in Kwakshua Channel, between Calvert and Hecate islands, and discuss the events of the last couple of days. It's a tossup between dolphins and humpbacks for the highest rating. Matkin hands me a report produced by his wife, Olga von Ziegesar, and researcher Beth Miller. They were asked by the National Marine Fisheries Service to examine the effects of the *Exxon Valdez* oil spill on humpback whales in Prince William Sound. Since humpbacks only begin to appear in the area in May, no humpbacks were seen swimming in the oil after the March 1989 spill, but they were later observed feeding in heavily oiled areas.

Summer populations of humpbacks have been studied in the sound since the mid-1970s. In 1990 von Ziegesar's team identified sixty-six individuals, including fifteen "new" whales, never seen before in Prince William Sound. A number of animals—"old-timers," as von Ziegesar calls them—returned in 1989 after the spill, and again the next year. Some were accompanied by calves and were feeding in areas through which large amounts of oil had passed.

"The condition of the humpback whale in Prince William Sound appears to be good. The number of animals using the Sound has remained fairly consistent despite the spill," say von Ziegesar and Miller. They note, however, that a humpback death is difficult to

FEEDING BIRDS SHARE A MEAL OF HERRING WITH A MINKE WHALE. RESEARCH SUGGESTS THESE WHALES RETURN TO THE SAME FEEDING AREAS EACH SUMMER. THE DORSAL FIN OF THE MINKE, THE SMALLEST BALEEN WHALE, CARRIES NICKS AND SCRATCHES WHICH HELP IDENTIFY INDIVIDUAL ANIMALS. THE SCARS ON THE SIDE OF THIS WHALE WERE PROBABLY MADE BY THE TEETH OF AN ORCA.

detect because they range so widely. They also warn it's too early for unbridled optimism.

"Immediate impacts on humpback whales from exposure to oil in Prince William Sound have not been observed, however it is very difficult to see the more insidious long-term effects, especially in a long-lived species like the humpback whale. Injuries, diseases, or reproductive failure resulting from inhalation or ingestion of either the crude oil or the chemicals that have been applied since the spill may not be apparent for years. Only by continued observation will we see the changes."

* * *

About seven hundred kilometres from Prince William Sound, whales in southeast Alaska blew away accepted theories on humpback migrations in the North Pacific. In

the late 1970s it was thought that humpbacks breeding in subtropical waters generally swam in a straight line north to summer feeding grounds. Hawaiian whales went to the Aleutians; Mexican whales swam to more easterly parts of Alaska. Little was known of Asian humpbacks that wintered at Bonin Island and in the Ryuku and Mariana islands. These were believed to be three separate populations.

In 1979, Jim Darling, who'd been photo-identifying humpbacks in Hawaii, flew to Juneau, Alaska, to meet Chuck and Virginia Jurasz, who'd been photographing Alaskan humpbacks for twelve years. They sat down with a pile of pictures and found a match on the third shot. Before the end of the day they'd matched seven whales.

"We thought, my God, throw out everything that we know about humpbacks in the Pacific and let's start again," Darling recalls. "This is the great rush. One of the rewards of being a researcher is learning something before everybody else in the world knows it. There's a bit of a charge to that."

Twelve years later, Darling got a similar charge when he discovered through photographs that a humpback seen in Japan in 1990 was seen in Hawaii in 1991. Photographs of more than two hundred Japanese humpbacks have been compared to thousands from the opposite side of the Pacific and this is the only match. The belief that Japan's population of five hundred to a thousand humpbacks is separate from those of the eastern Pacific may require rethinking.

Darling has continued working with humpback whales since he fell into a career with Hawaiian humpbacks by accident. He'd completed his master's field work on Vancouver Island gray whales and had been accepted to study grays in Mexico under Dr. Ken Norris, the "grandfather of whale research," at the University of California in Santa Cruz. He got sidetracked by one of his master's supervisors, Roger Payne, who had recently introduced the song of the humpback whale to the world.

At Payne's invitation, Darling went to Maui in 1977, set up house in an old boat at Lahaina, and began recording humpback songs. He did more recording the next year and started photo-identifying whales. By the end of 1979 he had amassed a file of 264 individual humpbacks. Researcher Dan McSweeney contributed another 95 humpbacks from the seas around the neighbouring island of Hawaii.

After their startling discovery in Alaska, Darling flew directly to Boston to see Payne, whose wife, Katy, had recently returned from Mexico's Revillagigedo Islands with eleven ID shots of humpback whales. Two matched Darling's pictures. Another theory blown away—the assumption that Hawaiian and Mexican whales didn't mix, that they always returned to the same wintering grounds. Later another whale that wintered in Hawaii one year was located in Mexico the next. The Hawaii-Mexico link was further tightened

A COW AND CALF SWIM FLUIDLY JUST BELOW THE SURFACE IN THE CRYSTAL BLUE WATERS OF HAWAII. CALVES MEASURING FOUR OR FIVE METRES LONG, WEIGHING NEARLY TWO TONNES, ARE BORN AFTER A TWELVE-MONTH GESTATION PERIOD. MANY HUMPBACK COWS BEAR A CALF EVERY YEAR, GIVING REASON FOR OPTIMISM ABOUT THE RECOVERY OF THE SPECIES.

when Payne, who believed that each whale population had its own song, heard Mexican whales singing the same tune as Hawaiian humpbacks.

"What that said, of course, was that if they were singing the same song, they're the same whales," says Darling. "That led to a paper by Roger suggesting the humpback song could be used as an indicator of stocks in the world. It led to just a whole different feeling for how humpbacks treat the North Pacific—it's sort of their back yard. Our whole concept of how whales function just went right out the window."

Along with it went Darling's Ph.D. studies of gray whales. Norris agreed he should continue his humpback work, studying their abundance, behaviour, and migrations. Major studies involving researchers in a number of teams were launched in Maui in 1980, with Darling the head of one team. "It was a very exciting time because we were learning a lot of stuff, working with a lot of very interested people."

The study teams were based in Lahaina, on the leeward side of the Hawaiian Islands, an area preferred by cows with calves, and by fairweather researchers in boats. Hundreds of humpbacks pass through these waters, staging spectacular courtship displays with breaching, spy-hopping, tail-lobbing, and, for those who can hear underwater, singing. The movement of whales is constant and, like the breeding gray whales of Baja, some Hawaiian humpbacks stay several weeks, others are gone within a few days. They move all around the Hawaiian Islands but, because of the calmer seas, these whales off Lahaina provide the best whale-watching and research opportunities.

Photo-identification was standard practice by the late 1970s. Graeme Ellis's expertise in the field was well known and he soon arrived with his family to help with photography. "The first year we had a house with fourteen or fifteen people living in it, all divided up with bamboo curtains for privacy," says Ellis, whose wife was pregnant with their second child.

"My job was to do photo-IDs and I photographed every whale in sight. Those whales would come and go through the season. They weren't always the same whales day to day; there was a constant influx. They probably move through the islands: they're certainly off all the other islands."

To try and interpret the significance of the humpback song, researchers on the water worked with a shore-based team who had a surveyor's theodolite and a computer at the top of a hill. They had figured out that a singing whale invariably surfaces at the same point in its repetitive song. When a singer was heard through a hydrophone, a report was radioed to the hilltop observers. When the song came to that certain point, they'd watch for a blow. The boaters would race over and shoot ID pictures while the observers recorded its movements and those of any whales around it.

While Ellis worked on the surface, Flip Nicklin would scuba dive as deep as forty metres

A SINGING HUMPBACK WHALE TYPICALLY POSITIONS ITSELF AT A FORTY-FIVE-DEGREE ANGLE ABOUT FIFTY METRES BELOW THE SURFACE. WITH PECTORAL FINS OUTSTRETCHED AND HEAD BOWED, IT SINGS SONGS COMPOSED OF TWO TO EIGHT SPECIFIC THEMES, ALWAYS IN THE SAME SEQUENCE. IT'S BELIEVED THESE EERIE SONGS ARE AN EXPRESSION OF DOMINANCE OR AGGRESSION.

AN AMOROUS BULL HUMPBACK (LEFT BACKGROUND) ATTEMPTS TO "ESCORT" A COW AND CALF. AFTER BATTLING OTHER BULLS FOR THE RIGHT TO COURT THIS COW, THE MALE WILL MATE WITH THE FEMALE, THEN PROBABLY SEARCH FOR ANOTHER PARTNER. THE TINY FISH IN THE FOREGROUND ARE FEEDING ON DEAD SKIN SHED BY THE WHALES.

to sex whales by photographing the undersides. As he approached a whale from below he'd hold his breath—and bubbles—then quickly shoot the tail and genital slit before exhaling.

The photographs helped confirm that only males sing. They position themselves within fifty metres of the surface, their bodies inclined at a forty-five-degree angle. With head bowed and pectoral fins outstretched, they sing songs composed of two to eight specific themes, always in the same sequence. Every ten or fifteen minutes they come up for air. Some whales sing only a few minutes; others chant their melancholy melodies for as long as seven hours.

Their songs can be likened to a variety of earthly noises—a bull elephant trumpeting through a tunnel, the low-pitched mooing of a cow, a humongous slide whistle, or a giant blowing his nose from the top of a bean stalk. Higher-pitched phrases may sound like orca calls, the bark of a sea lion, or the cry of a baby. They alternate between low and high-pitched themes, and a song is repeated many times through a singing session. These songs gradually change over time. Hearing one at close range is a decidedly eerie sensation.

Darling contends the song of a lone humpback whale is a secondary sexual characteristic used to help determine dominance among males competing for a female.

"I propose that the humpback 'song' is an acoustic display whose function is analogous to the visual displays of dominance of land mammals," he writes in his doctoral thesis. "An acoustic display is the only functional means of communicating one's dominance over any distance in the marine environment."

"Both horns and antlers, and 'song' are extraordinarily elaborate displays," he says. He points out that songs, like antlers, change with the animal's age and physical condition, and correlate with the whale's position in the dominance order. He also notes that their songs, like antlers, seem to grow as their hormones switch into gear. While the songs of all the singers in a population are strikingly similar, there are subtle differences which often are overlooked, Darling says, adding more study should be done on the relationship between a whale's song and the size of the animal. Many within the scientific fraternity feel Darling's hypothesis that humpback songs are analogous to antlers is farfetched.

Humpbacks emit other vocalizations distinct from singing, which appear related to competition for females. Scientist Peter Tyack, who worked with Darling in Maui, played these sounds underwater: some whales were attracted; others actually charged the speaker. When Tyack played recordings of songs to humpbacks, the whales in the area moved away. These reactions show how little is understood about the meaning of humpback whale vocalizations.

The researchers at Maui were the first to observe the courting rituals of humpback whales, but even today, after several years of intense scientific study above and below the surface, there are no documented observations of sexual intercourse between humpback whales. Mating humpbacks begin to show up at Hawaii in November and the numbers peak between February and April. A few stick around into late May and early June.

On the breeding grounds these acrobatic whales entertain thousands of tourists with their fluking, breaching, and spy-hopping. They leap from the water, twisting their thirty-five-tonne bodies in half-turns as they crash down. Breaching may be a form of communication, or a means of ridding their bodies of barnacles and parasites. Humpbacks have been documented breaching forty times in succession.

As these whales breach, they are easy to identify by their long, winglike foreflippers with scalloped edges. The pectoral fins of a full-grown humpback may measure five metres long, about a third of its total body length. The tops of their heads are spotted with sensitive tubercles, or wartlike bumps, each embellished by a single hair. Their skin is scarred, and barnacles cling to their chins, throats, and flippers. Deep grooves in their throats stretch down to their navels. About two-thirds of the way back from the head is a tiny dorsal fin, sitting on top of a small hump.

"Its shape, compared with the symmetrical forms of the Finback, California Gray, and Sulphurbottom, is decidedly ugly," wrote whaler Charles Scammon, "as it has a short, thick body, and frequently a diminutive 'small', with inordinately large pectorals and flukes."

On the mating grounds, mature males, about nine years old, are anything but gentle giants. They fight aggressively for the right to "escort" a cow and calf, not to protect the calf, but to copulate with the mother. There is often bloodshed among battling bulls: they smash each other with their tails, ram their opponents, and trumpet through their blowholes at the surface. Many males withdraw from these melees permanently scarred. A victorious escort may complete its business with its hard-won mate, then seek another partner.

These truculent males undergo an abrupt personality change once a female is chosen. "In the mating season they are noted for their amorous antics," wrote Scammon. "At such times their caresses are of the most amusing and novel character, and these performances have doubtless given rise to the fabulous tales of the sword-fish and thrasher attacking whales. When lying by the side of each other, the megapteras frequently administer alternate blows with their long fins, which love-pats may, on a still day, be heard at a distance of miles. They also rub each other with these same huge and flexible arms, rolling occasionally from side to side, and indulging in other gambols which can easier be imagined than described."

After a twelve-month gestation period, calves measuring four or five metres long, weighing nearly two tonnes, are born in these southern seas. One reason for optimism about the humpback's potential for recovery from early exploitation is that many cows bear a calf every year.

In their mating waters a few curious humpbacks approach boats, but they rarely exhibit "friendly" behaviour like gray whales. Ellis and his eight-year-old son, Jason, occasionally swam with whales in Hawaii. While climbing into the water Ellis once stepped onto the back of a humpback lying under the boat. Cows and calves were most approachable and he'd slip into the water with mask and snorkel and swim from a distance of about a hundred metres, trying not to spook the animals.

"Usually the calf would get curious and come up and have a look. The mom would be deeper down so we could just barely make her out. If we came between the calf and the mom and she saw us, we could almost see her jump. She'd turn and come straight at us usually, pick up the calf and leave.

"But they're always incredibly careful. They come at you and it looks like a flipper is going to bump right into you: they lift it up right over top of you then go back down the other side. As they go by, if their flukes are close to you, they'll stop pumping as they pass you, then turn on the power afterwards. You get caught up in the prop wash sometimes."

At the end of the calving season, their journeys to winter feeding waters begin. While

HUMPBACKS ARE EASILY RECOG-
NIZED BY THEIR LONG, WINGLIKE
FOREFLIPPERS WITH SCALLOPED
EDGES. THEY LOOK MUCH LIKE
THE SERRATED EDGES OF A
CARPENTER'S SAW. THE PEC-
TORAL FINS OF A FULL-GROWN
HUMPBACK MAY MEASURE FIVE
METRES LONG, ABOUT A THIRD
OF ITS TOTAL BODY LENGTH.

151 HUMPBACKS, MINKES AND
MISCELLANY

some travel more than five thousand kilometres across the open ocean to the Gulf of Alaska or Bering Sea, others follow the coastline for two thousand kilometres from the Revillagigedo Islands to central California. Like gray whales, humpbacks prefer the shallow, productive seas of the continental shelf. Several hundred are seen each year foraging in California waters.

Monterey Bay has always been well known to humpback observers. Nineteenth-century whalers knew when to expect whales and, even without the aid of photo-identification, some animals became familiar by their markings. "One of the largest of these whales having an unusual mark—a white spot on the hump—was recognized for several years in succession in its periodical migrations with the rest of its wandering companions, and the time of passing Point Pinos (the outer headland of the bay), was ascertained to be during or near the month of September," wrote Captain Scammon. "Repeated efforts were made, from year to year, to capture the member of the 'gam' thus distinguished by the white hump; but it was only when the bomb-gun and bomb-lance had come into use that its destruction was effected."

Fortunately for Humphrey the wayward whale, twentieth-century attitudes were not so profit-motivated. Humphrey became famous after taking a detour up the Sacramento River. First seen in San Francisco Bay on October 10, 1985, this humpback swam upstream into the San Joaquin-Sacramento delta, many kilometres from the ocean, and biologists were worried it would die in fresh water. A costly, heavily publicized rescue mission was mounted to lure Humphrey back to sea. On November 4, three and a half weeks and $92,000 later, the wandering whale passed under the Golden Gate Bridge and headed for the open ocean.

Humphrey was photographed during the next three years in the Gulf of the Farallons National Marine Sanctuary. The sanctuary, established by President Jimmy Carter in 1981, encompasses 3,223 square kilometres of ocean from Bodega Head to Rocky Point and includes the waters within a twenty-two-kilometre radius of the Farallon National Wildlife Refuge. Ken Balcomb, with colleagues John Calambokidis and Jim Cubbage, studied abundance, distribution, and behaviour of humpbacks in the sanctuary.

During three seasons from 1986 to '88 there were over a thousand humpback sightings, most in August when there's an influx of the species into the sanctuary. A total of 225 individuals were identified. By matching pictures they found that 23 of these whales had been in Mexico, 2 came from Costa Rica, and 3 from Hawaii. Humpbacks were usually seen in water between sixty and ninety metres deep, feeding on euphausiids and anchovies.

The researchers returned in 1989 and '90 and photographed more humpbacks, raising the total identified in the sanctuary to 333. Balcomb and Diane Claridge also photo-

A CURIOUS HUMPBACK CALF AP-
PROACHES THE UNDERWATER
CAMERA OF GRAEME ELLIS, WHO
WAS SNORKELLING OFF LAHAI-
NA. WHEN ELLIS CAME BETWEEN
THE CALF AND ITS MOTHER, THE
PROTECTIVE COW DARTED UP
FROM THE DEPTHS AND SCUR-
RIED AWAY WITH ITS OFFSPRING,
LEAVING A STARTLED ELLIS
DRIFTING ALONE ON THE
SURFACE.

A LAZY HUMPBACK LOLLS IN THE HAWAIIAN SUN. BARNACLES ARE PARTICULARLY NOTICEABLE ON THE TIPS OF THE FLUKES AND PECTORAL FINS OF HUMPBACKS. NOT ALL WHALE SPECIES HOST BARNACLES, BUT THOSE THAT DO EACH HAVE THEIR OWN PARTICULAR BRAND OF BARNACLES. ON THE HUMPBACK, THREE DIFFERENT SPECIES GROW ON THE FINS, FLUKES, THROAT, AND CHIN.

identified 24 humpbacks in Oregon and Washington between June and September, 1990: 5 of those whales subsequently appeared in the Gulf of the Farallons in October and November.

Balcomb's team also examined blue whales in the sanctuary from 1986 to '90. These whales feed almost exclusively on krill and pelagic red crabs. During the study they were commonly seen with concentrations of marine birds, notably Cassin's auklets and phalaropes. A total of 284 were identified in the gulf, along with another 88 outside the sanctuary at Monterey Bay. One blue whale in the gulf was originally identified in 1975. Many of these blue whales winter off the coast of Baja and Central America and 42 photographed in California were also identified in Mexico.

Some scientists say there were probably five thousand blue whales in the North Pacific at the turn of the century. Exceptionally fast swimmers, they weren't exploited until the advent of steam and diesel power, and explosive harpoons. Like humpbacks, they came close to extinction before they were protected in 1966. Today there may be two thousand in the North Pacific, where they range seasonally from Panama to the Chukchi Sea.

Although blues and humpbacks share much of the same ocean, the movements of humpback whales have received more attention. Humpback whales don't form orca-type pods, but there is evidence that the same whales often hang out together. There have been instances where whales seen together in Alaska were seen with one another in Hawaii. There is also proof that many whales return to the same feeding waters each year. At least fifty known whales regularly travel between Hawaii and the Alexander Archipelago in southeast Alaska. In 1980 a humpback seen feeding off Swiftsure Bank, near the entrance to Juan de Fuca Strait, was also seen at Hawaii in the winters of 1980 and '81. The same whale was seen again at Swiftsure Bank in 1989.

"The whales are simply found in the most productive places," says Darling. "There's no magic about it. So if whales are repeatedly seen in the same area, such as Swiftsure or La Perouse banks, where they have been seen forever, they're obviously incredibly productive areas."

Humpbacks in the waters off Vancouver Island were once the most abundant species. They were the mainstay of several whaling stations that processed whales taken from inside waters and from the long fjords that penetrate the mainland mountains. Those whales, the ones closest to home, were the first to go: by 1907 humpback whales had vanished from Georgia Strait.

Graeme Ellis speculates that humpbacks learn of the best feeding waters from their mothers during their first year of life. But when the whales that came to the inside waters were wiped out, these highly productive areas were forgotten. "I don't know how long it takes for a cow to come in with a calf, to rediscover that this is great feeding."

By the late 1970s and early '80s, reports of humpbacks in inside waters began to surface. Small numbers were being seen at the mouths of fjords, in harbours, and in the middle of Georgia Strait. As humpback numbers grow it's likely that more will learn that Georgia Strait and other inside waters are still extremely productive.

Pacific gray whales have had at least twenty years longer than humpbacks to recover. If gray whales are an example, and if we humans have the sense to keep our oceans intact, there's reason for optimism about the humpback's future throughout the North Pacific.

"I think the humpbacks are coming back," says Ellis. "I don't see any reason why they won't."

BARNACLES, SEAWEED, AND OTHER GROWTH ARE EXPOSED TO THE SUN AS A BREACHING HUMPBACK LANDS ON ITS BACK. THESE PLANTS AND ANIMALS GROW IN THE THROAT GROOVES, WHICH EXTEND AS FAR AS THE NAVEL AND EXPAND AS THE WHALE SWALLOWS ITS PREY. PERHAPS BREACHING IS A WHALE'S WAY OF TRYING TO RID ITSELF OF PARASITES.

Epilogue

Since research on wild whales began in the early 1970s, perhaps the most significant revelation is that these great leviathans can, in fact, be studied in their own oceans. It isn't such an outlandish proposition after all. And though they spend most of their lives out of human sight, we've amassed volumes of information based on the comparatively little time they spend sharing our air in the terrestrial world. We've learned even more by invading their domain, by eavesdropping with hydrophones, or slipping underwater and swimming alongside big bull whales or cautious cows with calves, something no person would have dared to contemplate only a few decades ago.

The dissection of whales on the slipways of whaling stations has contributed to the understanding of cetacean anatomy and diet. Experiments and observations of captive whales have, and still do, provide invaluable insights into their behaviour, dietary and medical needs, and personality traits. But harpooned and captive whales are not the real world, and that realization has progressed beyond the academic community. The public today would be outraged at the thought of killing a whale, any whale, for scientific research. And as we approach the twenty-first century, a worldwide ban on the live capture of wild whales is a probability, if not a certainty. A complete turnaround in only two decades: future knowledge of whales will be derived almost entirely from the study of wild animals.

Many, if not most, of the major breakthroughs happened in the 1970s and '80s,

BLOOD AND WATER STREAM FROM THE FLUKES OF A HUMPBACK WHALE. BARNACLES THAT EMBED THEMSELVES IN THE WHALE'S SKIN MAY CAUSE BLEEDING WHEN THEY'RE KNOCKED OFF. THIS WHALE REPEATEDLY SLAPPED ITS TAIL ON THE SURFACE, WHIPPING THE SEA INTO A FRENZY OF FOAM, BEFORE QUIETLY SLIPPING FROM OUR WORLD INTO ITS OWN.

understandably so when one considers how little was known of wild whales before then. Simple logistics—ironing out the kinks—occupied much of the first few years: surviving and working in remote field camps for two to four months; contending, like all mariners, with inclement weather; predicting the unpredictability of whales.

There is no question the most important early development was photo-identification. It has allowed researchers to distinguish one pod from another, one whale from another, to follow migrations across the open Pacific, to determine the calving frequency of cows, and to see that each whale has its idiosyncrasies. Researchers soon learned that photo-identification varies from species to species. Killer whales are recognized by dorsal fins and saddle patches, gray whales by distinctive patterns on their backs, humpbacks by the undersides of their flukes.

The fact that each species cannot be photo-identified by the same technique lends credence to the assumption that what we learn about one can't always be extrapolated to another. The complexities of killer-whale societies are unheard-of in the entire mammal kingdom, let alone among cetaceans. The bottom-scouring methods of feeding gray whales are unique in the world of whales. The songs of amorous humpbacks set them apart from all other cetaceans. The environmental requirements of these and other species vary with their habits and habitats.

Despite all this headway, wild-whale research is still in its infancy. The foundations have been laid; there is a proven need for ongoing monitoring of Pacific whale populations. With some whales living seventy or eighty years, it would be ridiculous to conclude that we understand them after twenty years, a quarter of one old whale's lifetime. But monitoring now is routine: it is time for more creative research. DNA fingerprinting, whale societies, vocalizations and behaviours, regional differences among the same species: this work has begun, and those at the forefront of today's science must cultivate new researchers to carry on—it's a never-ending task.

It is also time for a harder look beyond the animals to the habitat. While we discuss the environmental needs of whales, we continue to blanket the ocean floor with effluent from pulp mills and other industries. While we attempt to calculate the amount of salmon a killer whale needs to survive, we systematically destroy the spawning streams by clearcut logging. While we talk of promoting public awareness through whale-watching, we overlook the increasing noise pollution we bring to the sea.

These difficult problems are being addressed, but many prominent whale researchers worry they will not be solved in time to ensure a promising future for our whales. There is an urgency as we stride toward the turn of a new century: perhaps it is time to take a broader view, a more responsible look at the havoc we humans wreak on our oceans.

Metric Conversions

Here is a simple table to help you understand the metric system:

WHEN YOU KNOW	MULTIPLY BY	TO FIND
centimetres	.4	inches
metres	3.3	feet
kilometres	.63	miles
square metres	1.25	square yards
square kilometres	.4	square miles
hectares	2.5	acres
kilograms	2.2	pounds

OR:

inches	2.5	centimetres
feet	.3	metres
miles	1.6	kilometres
square yards	.8	square metres
square miles	2.6	square kilometres
acres	.4	hectares
pounds	.45	kilograms

FAHRENHEIT/
CELSIUS

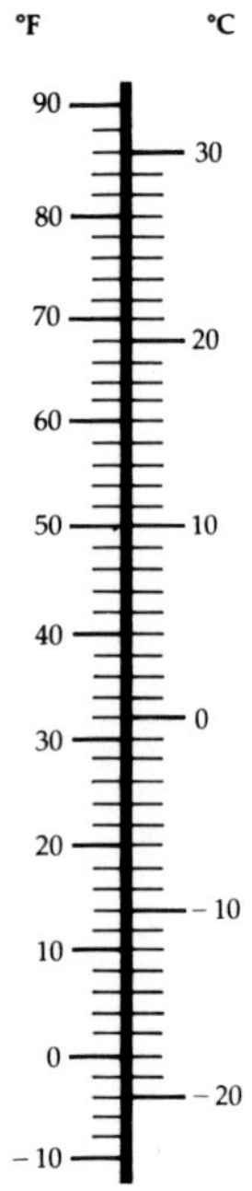

Temperatures are given in Celsius and their relationship to the Fahrenheit scale is shown at right.

Bibliography

Balcomb, K. C. III. "Kith and Kin of the Killer Whale." San Francisco, CA: *Pacific Discovery*, Vol. 44, No. 2, Spring 1991.

Barnes, Lawrence G. and McLeod, Samuel A. "The Fossil Record and Phyletic Relationships of Gray Whales." Orlando, Florida: Academic Press, Inc., 1984.

Bigg, Michael A. et al. *Killer Whales*. Nanaimo, B.C.: Phantom Press & Publishers Inc., 1987.

_____. "Social Organization and Genealogy of Resident Killer Whales in the Coastal Waters of British Columbia and Washington State." Cambridge, U.K.: International Whaling Commission, Special Issue 12, 1990.

Calambokidis, John et al. "Biology of Blue Whales in the Gulf of the Farallones and Adjacent Areas of California." Olympia, WA: Cascadia Research Collective, 1989.

_____. "Biology of Humpback Whales in the Gulf of the Farallones." Olympia, WA: Cascadia Research Collective, 1989.

_____. "Research on Humpback and Blue Whales in the Gulf of the Farallones and Adjacent Waters, 1989 and 1990." Olympia, WA: Casacadia Research Collective, 1991.

Coerr, Eleanor and Evans, William E. *Gigi: A Baby Whale Borrowed for Science and Returned to the Sea*. New York, NY: G. P. Putnam's Sons, 1980.

Cook, Joseph J. and Wisner, William L. *Killer Whale!* New York, NY: Dodd, Mead & Company, 1963.

Dahlheim, Marilyn E. et al. "Sound Production by the Gray Whale and Ambient Noise Levels in Laguna San Ignacio, Baja California Sur, Mexico." Orlando, Florida: Academic Press, Inc., 1984.

Darling, Jim. "Survey for Nestucca Oil Sediments of Selected Gray Whale Feeding Sites." Ottawa, Ont.: Department of Fisheries and Oceans, 1989.

_____. *Wild Whales*. Vancouver, B.C.: SummerWild Productions, 1987.

_____. "Gray Whales off Vancouver Island." Victoria, B.C.: University of Victoria, 1984.

_____. "Migrations, Abundance and Behaviour of Hawaiian Humpback Whales." Santa Cruz, CA: University of Santa Cruz, 1983.

Dorsey, Eleanor M. "Exclusive Adjoining Ranges in Individually Identified Minke Whales (*Balaenoptera acutorostrata*) in Washington State." Ottawa, Ont.: National Research Council, 1983.

Dorsey, Eleanor M. et al. "Minke Whales (*Balaenoptera acutorostrata*) from the West Coast of North America: Individual Recognition and Small-Scale Site Fidelity." Lincoln, MA: Long Term Research Institute, 1991.

Fisheries and Oceans, Dept. of. "Guidelines for Whale Watching." Ottawa, Ont.: 1986.

_____. "Johnstone Strait Killer Whale Committee, Background Report." Ottawa, Ont.: 1991.

Ford, John K. B. "Family Fugues." New York, NY: *Natural History,* March, 1991.

Francis, Daniel. *A History of World Whaling.* Markham, Ont.: Viking, 1990.

Griffin, Edward I. "Making Friends with a Killer Whale." Washington, D.C.: *National Geographic,* Vol. 129, No.3, March, 1966.

Haley, Delphine et al. *Marine Mammals of Eastern North Pacific and Arctic Waters.* Seattle, WA: Pacific Search Press, 1986.

Hall, Howard. "Eye to Eye with a Gray Whale." Vienna, VA: National Wildlife Federation, from *International Wildlife* magazine, May/June 1985.

Harrison, Sir Richard et al. *Whales, Dolphins and Porpoises.* Hong Kong: Intercontinental Publishing Corporation Ltd., 1988.

Henderson, David A. "Nineteenth Century Gray Whaling: Grounds, Catches and Kills, Practices and Depletion of the Whale Population." Orlando, Florida: Academic Press, Inc., 1984.

Hoelzel, A. Rus. "Analysis of Regional Mitochondrial DNA Variation in the Killer Whale; Implications for Cetacean Conservation." Cambridge, U.K.: University of Cambridge, 1991.

Hoelzel, A. Rus et al. "Mitochondrial D-loop DNA Variation Within and Between Populations of Minke Whale (*Balaenoptera acutorostrata*)." Cambridge, U.K.: University of Cambridge, 1991.

_____. "A Paternity Test Case for the Killer Whale (*Orcinus orca*) by DNA Fingerprinting." Cambridge, U.K.: Society for Marine Mammalogy, 1991.

_____. "Genetic Differentiation between Sympatric Killer Whale Populations." Cambridge, U.K.: University of Cambridge, 1990.

_____. "The Foraging Specializations of Individual Minke Whales." Lincoln, MA: Long Term Research Institute, 1989.

Hoyt, Erich. *Orca, The Whale Called Killer.* Camden East, Ont.: Camden House, revised 1990.

Hunter, Robert. *Warriors of the Rainbow: A Chronicle of the Greenpeace Movement.* New York, NY: Holt, Rinehart and Winston, 1979.

Jones, Mary Lou. "The Reproductive Cycle in Gray Whales Based on Photographic Resightings of Females on the Breeding Grounds from 1977-82." San Diego, CA: Cetacean Research Associates, 1988.

Jones, Mary Lou et al. *The Gray Whale.* Orlando, Florida: Academic Press, Inc., 1984.

Jones, Mary Lou and Swartz, Steven L. "Demography and Phenology of Gray Whales and Evaluation of Whale-Watching Activities in Laguna San Ignacio, Baja California Sur, Mexico." Orlando, Florida: Academic Press, Inc., 1984.

Krupnick, Igor I. "Gray Whales and the Aborigines of the Pacific Northwest: The History of Aboriginal Whaling." Orlando, Florida: Academic Press, Inc., 1984.

Leatherwood, Stephen et al. *Whales, Dolphins, and Porpoises of the Eastern North Pacific and Adjacent Waters.* New York, NY: Dover Publications, Inc., 1988.

_____. "Cetaceans of the Channel Islands National Marine Sanctuary." Washington, D.C.: National Oceanic and Atmospheric Administration, 1987.

Mate, Bruce R. and Harvey, James T. "Ocean Movements of Radio-Tagged Gray Whales." Orlando, Florida: Academic Press, Inc., 1984.

Markin, Craig O. "Killer Whale Interactions with the Sablefish Longline Fishery in Prince William Sound, Alaska 1985, with Comments on the Bering Sea." Juneau, AK: National Marine Fisheries Service, 1986.

Matkin, Craig O. and Ellis, Graeme. "The Status of Killer Whales in Prince William Sound in 1990." Seattle, WA: National Marine Fisheries Service, 1990.

McIntyre, Joan. _Mind in the Waters._ Toronto, Ont.: McClelland and Stewart Ltd., 1974.

Morton, Alexandra B. _Siwiti—A Whale's Story._ Victoria, B.C.: Orca Book Publishers, 1991.

_____. "A Quantitative Comparison of the Behaviour of Resident and Transient Forms of the Killer Whale off the Central British Columbia Coast." Cambridge, U.K.: International Whaling Commission, Special Issue 12, 1988.

Nerini, Mary. "A Review of Gray Whale Feeding Ecology." Orlando, Florida: Academic Press, Inc., 1984.

Nichol, Linda M. "Seasonal Movements and Foraging Behaviour of Resident Killer Whales in Relation to the Inshore Distribution of Salmon in British Columbia." Vancouver, B.C.: University of B.C., 1990.

Obee, Bruce. "The Great Killer Whale Debate." Vanier, Ont.: _Canadian Geographic,_ Vol. 112, No. 1, Jan./Feb. 1992.

_____. _Coastal Wildlife of British Columbia._ Vancouver, B.C.: Whitecap Books Ltd., 1991.

_____. "Probing Our Undersea Frontier." Vanier, Ont.: _Canadian Geographic,_ Vol. 111, No. 3, June/July 1991.

_____. "Gentle Giants." Vanier, Ont.: _Canadian Geographic,_ Vol. 110, No. 6, Dec. 90/Jan. 1991.

_____. "Strip Mining the Seas." Vanier, Ont.: _Canadian Geographic,_ Vol. 110, No. 1, Feb./March 1990.

_____. _The Pacific Rim Explorer_ Vancouver, B.C.: Whitecap Books Ltd., 1986.

O'Leary, Beth Laura. "Aboriginal Whaling from the Aleutian Islands to Washington State." Orlando, Florida: Academic Press, Inc., 1984.

Olesiuk, Peter et al. "Life History and Population Dynamics of Resident Killer Whales in the Coastal Waters of British Columbia and Washington State." Ottawa, Ont.: Department of Fisheries and Oceans, 1988.

Palmer, Mark J. "Tales Told by the Tail of a Whale." San Francisco, CA: _Pacific Discovery,_ Vol. 40, No. 3, July/Sept. 1987.

Payne, Katy B. "A Change of Tune." New York, NY: _Natural History,_ March, 1991.

Poole, Mike. _Island of Whales._ Vancouver, B.C.: Island of Whales Productions Ltd. Distributed by National Film Board of Canada, Central Television Enterprises, 1990.

Reeves, Randall R. "Modern Commercial Pelagic Whaling for Gray Whales." Orlando, Florida: Academic Press, Inc., 1984.

Sayers, Hazel. "Shore Whaling for Gray Whales along the Coast of the Californias." Orlando, Florida: Academic Press, Inc., 1984.

Scammon, Charles M. *The Marine Mammals of the Northwestern Coast of North America*. San Francisco, CA: John H. Carmany and Company, 1874.

Spong, Paul. "Corky Come Home." Bristol, U.K.: *BBC Wildlife*, Vol. 9, No. 3, March, 1991.

Stern, S. Jonathan et al. "Photographic Catchability of Individually Identified Minke Whales (*Balaenoptera acutorostrata*) of the San Juan Islands, Washington and the Monterey Bay Area, California." San Francisco State University, 1991.

Swartz, Steven L. "Gray Whale Migration, Social and Breeding Behavior." San Diego, CA: Cetacean Research Associates, 1986.

_____. "Gray Whales (*Eschrichtius robustus*) in Laguna San Ignacio, Baja California Sur, Mexico: 1978-1982." Washington, D.C.: National Geographic Society, 1985.

_____. "Cleaning Symbiosis Between Topsmelt, *Atherinops affinis*, and Gray Whale, *Eschrichtius robustus*, in Laguna San Ignacio, Baja California Sur, Mexico." San Diego, CA: Cetacean Research Associates, 1981.

Swartz, Steven L. and Jones, Mary Lou. "Gray Whales at Play in Baja's San Ignacio Lagoon." Washington, D.C.: National Geographic Society, Vol. 171, No. 6, June 1987.

_____. "Radio-Telemetric Studies of Gray Whale Migration along the California Coast: a Preliminary Comparison of Day and Night Migration Rates." San Diego, CA: Cetacean Research Associates, 1987.

_____. "Mothers and Calves," Stamford, CT: *Oceans*, March 1984.

_____. "Gray Whale (*Eschrichtius robustus*) Calf Production and Mortality in the Winter Range." San Diego, CA: Cetacean Research Associates, 1983.

Vancouver Public Aquarium. "The Humpback Whales of Georgia Strait." Vancouver, B.C.: *Journal of the Vancouver Aquarium*, Vol. 8, 1985.

Von Ziegesar, Olga and Miller, Beth. "Humpback Whale Survey in Prince William Sound, Alaska, 1990, After the *Exxon Valdez* Oil Spill." Seattle, WA: National Marine Fisheries Service, 1991.

White, Don et al. "Visual Acuity of the Killer Whale." Vancouver, B.C.: University of British Columbia, 1971.

Whittell, Giles. *The Story of Three Whales*. Vancouver, B.C.: Douglas and McIntyre, 1988.

Index